Your Dog's Life

Also by Deborah Loven Gray

The Great New York Dog Book

Your Dog's Life

RAISING, TRAINING, AND CARING FOR YOUR PET
FROM PUPPYHOOD TO OLD AGE

Deborah Loven Gray

HarperCollins*Publishers*

HarperCollins books may be purchased for educational, business, or sales promotional use. For information please write: Special Markets Department, HarperCollins Publishers, Inc., 10 East 53rd Street, New York, NY 10022.

FIRST EDITION

Designed by Elina D. Nudelman

Library of Congress Cataloging-in-Publication Data

Gray, Deborah Loven, 1963–
    Your dog's life : raising, training, and caring for your pet from
puppyhood to old age / Deborah Loven Gray. — 1st ed.
      p.   cm.
    ISBN 0-06-017391-2
    1. Dogs. I. Title.
SF427.G75   1997
636.7'0887—dc21   97-1903

97 98 99 00 01 ❖/RRD 10 9 8 7 6 5 4 3 2 1

To my husband, Josh, who has learned to love dogs
(and tolerate the parrots and horses who also share our life)

Contents

Contents

Acknowledgments

I wish to thank the many generous dog lovers whose enthusiasm and support guided this book: trainers Robin Kovary, Jody Potter, Sue Sternberg, George Quinlan, and Roy Hunter; breeders Ruth Anderson, Robbie Kaman at Fidelco Guide Dog Foundation, and the staff of Guiding Eyes for the Blind; veterinarians Dr. Gene Solomon, Dr. Sarah Garland, and Dr. Jim Hermann; Honey Loring of Camp Gone to the Dogs; wonderful photographer Jenny Eddy; the staff of the American Kennel Club Library; my New York "angels," Robert Jones, Pam Bernstein, and Phyllis Levy; and, of course, my family.

German shepherd Andrew's sable coat is similar in pigmentation to the coat of many wolves. *Courtesy of the author*

Preface

The Wolf at Your Side

As I sit writing with Serena dozing by my feet, it is easy to imagine that a wolf has found a place at my side. A large black and reddish-tan German shepherd, Serena is like her wild ancestors in many ways. Her ears stand erect. Her tail sweeps low when relaxed and comes up expressively to signal excitement or give a warning. Her coat is a wolffian coat: a thick, soft undercoat covered by longer, coarser guard hairs. Although she is the classic German shepherd black and tan, her cousin Andrew is a deep-red sable, her half brother Tristan is all black, and his littermate Spencer a light tannish gray: the same coat colors wolves wear.

Serena speaks with a wolf's voice, from the insistent "Let's go outside" whine to a low, warning growl. While she doesn't howl at the moon, Serena's vocal sister Calypso sings enough for both of them, lifting her muzzle to the sky to "answer" the calls of the police siren and fire truck.

Bred for a stable temperament and socialized from birth, Serena is friendly when introduced to strangers. Yet she has retained enough wolflike suspicion to effectively guard her home and her pack. Fortunately, she is free of another wild wolf ancestor trait: avoidance or shyness of humans. This timidity helps the wolf keep his distance from man, but is frustrating when it appears in a domesticated dog.

Like her wolffian grandams who killed to survive, Serena is thrilled by the hunt. She stalks squirrels, sneaking up on them slowly, then attacking with a burst of speed. Other dogs stalk and chase bicycle or car tires in the same way, using their wolffian hunting skills on less appropriate objects in their environment.

Wolves, and dogs, are scavengers as well as hunters. They will sample almost anything they come across that might make a meal. If a dead bird proves to be a little too old, they can regurgitate it effortlessly and go on their way none the worse for wear. Calypso is a real scavenger. From cups of coffee to dead skunks, Callie will try anything and usually like it.

My dog's most profound instincts come to her from wolves. When Serena was pregnant, she did her best to dig a den for her family, as her lupine foremothers would have. This meant burying into the piles of shoes and dresses that had slipped off hangers in the back of my closet, but it felt right to her.

When the puppies were born, she and the other dogs in our house behaved exactly as a wolf pack would have. All the members are involved with puppy raising. The mother is usually the alpha, or dominant female, and a talented huntress. Her skills are needed for the pack's survival. Soon after the cubs are born, she rejoins the hunt, leaving them in the care of a subordinate female, returning only for feedings. The "baby-sitter" is so attentive that naturalists studying wolf packs are frequently confused about which female wolf is the actual mother. As the pups become more mobile and harder to monitor, other pack members join in the puppy-minding, keeping

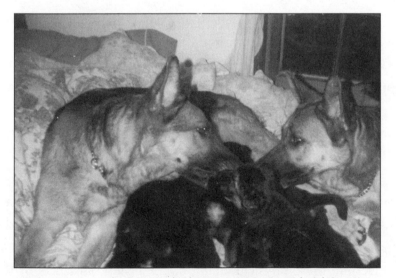

Which one is the mother? Serena *(left)* and her sister Calypso *(right)* share the babysitting duties for Serena's litter. *Courtesy of the author*

the inquisitive and energetic babies out of harm's way and teaching them the lessons they will need in order to survive.

Serena took full advantage of this system. She mothered her puppies, but considered her "career" as my shadow of equal importance. If I was going somewhere, she was with me, pups or no pups. Like the subordinate female wolf, sister Calypso stepped in for puppy duty. Eyes closed in blissful reverie, she would groom-lick her wriggly nieces and nephews for hours. As the puppies grew, cousin Andrew joined Calli in the care-taking, fussing, and watching over the inquisitive babies.

Why do my dogs act like wolves? Because genetically they are wolves, both wolves and dogs possessing seventy-eight chromosomes. The two species are still capable of cross-breeding, creating "wolf hybrids."

Thousands of years ago, man began to tame and breed wolves, slowly transforming them into the domestic dog. These "first friends" helped ancient man hunt, guarded his property, pulled loads, and drove his herds, the same jobs we ask our dogs to do today. As civilization evolved, the jobs dogs were needed for became more varied and specific and the different breeds were created to do those jobs.

Human-imposed genetic manipulation squashed the pug's nose to suit the fashion of the day, gave the rottweiler his mas-sive, deep chest to help him pull heavy loads, and designed the greyhound to run like a deer in order to catch his prey.

Despite these physical changes, the genetic instincts of the wolf—the prey drive, mothering, pack behavior and domi-nance, and all the rest—drive the dog. Beagle or rottweiler, shih tzu or pug, you're always looking at a wolf. For this reason it's helpful for the dog lover to become more familiar with *"canis père."*

Wolves and dogs live in pack societies that allow for individual development. They have group rituals such as greetings and leave-takings, feeding, playing, mating, and the all-important cooperative activity—hunting. They communicate with each other articulately and effortlessly through facial expressions and body movements. Vocalizations such as whines, growls, and howls are used, but wolves (and dogs) primarily speak body language.

Leading each wolf pack is a dominant male and female: the so-called alpha wolves. Under them, in a more fluid hierarchy, are other adolescent, young adult, and mature males and females who are sometimes related to the alphas. Elder wolves, who may have been alphas, can be present as well.

Usually the alpha wolves simply lead by example. Other pack members show them respect and submission, but voluntarily, like the protocol surrounding royalty. Following the initial power struggle that won the alpha his or her position, interwolf aggression is usually between lower-ranking members either trying to advance their position or hold on to the ranking they've achieved.

Much has been made about "becoming your dog's alpha." But the subtlety of the alpha wolf's role is important for dog owners to understand. Secure in their leadership abilities, alphas exude an air of authority. They don't need to behave aggressively to show their status. Similarly, you become your dog's leader by acting secure in your authority and enforcing the boundaries he needs to live with you, *not* by beating him into submission.

I prefer to view my relationship with Serena as one of "complementary companions" rather than as an alpha hierarchy. Obviously, in the human world I cause her to live in, I must be her leader. My environment contains things that are potentially dangerous to dogs—speeding cars, poisonous antifreeze, anti-roaming and dangerous-dog laws—and it would be irresponsible not to offer her leadership. But when we are in Serena's world, following a track through the woods or scaling obstacles on an agility course, or when she is growling into the black night at an unseen intruder outside our home, I follow her lead. Our relationship is about working together, as complementary companions, to build a life together.

While you must be your dog's leader—alpha, if you insist— it is to offer him necessary guidance.

What happens to old alpha wolves? Do they just "fade away," as old soldiers are supposed to do? Surprisingly, their fate seems to be directly related to how wisely, or justly, they ruled. Pack cohesion depends on subservient members accepting their positions and not challenging authority. An alpha is only an alpha if others *choose* to follow his or her leadership. Eventually, fair and permissive alphas are naturally replaced by a younger leader-type pack member. Like elder statesmen, these old alphas often remain in the pack in a position of honor.

But some alphas abuse their power. By harshly or randomly disciplining subservient wolves, suppressing their expressions of affection or play, the alpha can rule with an iron fist. Eventually, submissive members get fed up and stop acquiescing to the alpha's dominance. When revolution finally comes, it's not pretty. The deposition of such an alpha in a wolf pack causes violent fights that can last for days. Near the end, when it becomes clear that he or she will be deposed, the alpha is often "scapegoated": Members of *both* sexes turn on him or her. Even among wolves, karma is a boomerang.

A remarkably similar story was told to me by a breeder of Wheaten terriers. In a multiple-dog household, her old bitch was the alpha leader. A despot, she demanded complete submission at all times from the rest of the pack. Snarling and snapping, she would bully any dog who dared to play or relax in her presence. As she aged, her young daughters stayed at home, replacing her as breed dogs. The pack dynamic began to change as the daughters began refusing to submit to their mother. Rather than allow them to replace her, the old bitch attacked her daughters for their insubordination.

Facing constant vet bills, the breeder was forced to keep her dogs completely separate. This worked until she went away on vacation, leaving a friend to stay at her home. Although strict orders had been given to keep the old bitch separated, the friend felt sorry for the old girl and let all the dogs outside together to "play." Immediately, the old bitch was attacked by one of her daughters, and then all the dogs joined in against her with a vengeful fury. They killed her quickly.

The fate of despotic alphas within wolf packs should serve as a warning to dog owners who choose to treat their animals brutally. Eventually, like the submissive wolves, such dogs will somehow strike back.

Wolves, like dogs, learn about the world through experience: how to interact with the other pack members; what other animals are prey; which things in their environment are dangerous. Mature pack members supervise the young, helping them learn these lessons.

All of this knowledge is critical. No creature would last long in the wild without survival skills, and pack cohesion depends on each member wolf accepting his or her position within the group and working together as a team to survive.

As I've mentioned, the alphas are usually the "breeding pair" in the pack. The alpha female comes into season once a year, and evidence suggests that her mate only produces sperm during that time. We also believe that adult males and females in the pack of lower standing may not produce sperm or enter estrus at all while in subordinate pack positions. When these individuals leave the pack and find mates of their own, they become fertile.

This an important point for owners of pet dogs to consider. Nature takes the combustible force of sex out of the equation in a stable wolf pack. If lower-ranking pack members don't experience the drives of sex, they are less likely to challenge their superiors and will continue to work together for the pack's survival. Like an alpha wolf, a dog owner has to be his or her dog's leader. Neutering or spaying your pet removes the

same incendiary drive, making it easier for him to accept his position as your follower.

If hunting is good, the alpha wolves will mate, producing a litter of pups. In lean times, wolves seem to be able to practice birth control. While the fertility of a female wolf is undoubtedly linked to her overall health, it's interesting to see that wolves are unlikely to bring pups into the world unless they have a good chance of providing for them.

In each litter of wolf pups (or dog puppies) there is a range of individual temperaments. No pack could be made up of all leader wolves or all followers. A healthy mix is needed, and differences are appreciated and recognized in wolf packs. The play tussles of same-gender pups and adolescents help them figure out where they stand in relationship to their peers (captain of the football team or water boy).

More submissive members usually accept subservient social positions without incident. Go-getters eventually refuse to be submissive, and stir things up or leave their family pack. Naturalists who follow the social rankings and changes in wild packs often see an alpha male seek out a bold young male who shows leader-role potential, mentoring him as he matures.

The important thing about this for the dog owner is the realization that in *every* dog litter there is a range of genetically predetermined personality traits. Be realistic about your own leadership abilities and choose wisely, or let the breeder who knows her dogs choose for you. All puppies ARE NOT alike.

While wolf behavior is a wonderful guide to many of the drives within our own dogs, we did, after all, create a different animal when we domesticated dogs. How are they different? Primarily, we took a wild creature who was naturally timid and shy of humans—who would avoid contact if at all possible—and turned it into one who craves our company.

As I'll discuss in later chapters, a dog's attachment to humans is also influenced by his life experiences: the socialization he receives during his first year when he forms his opinion of the world, and subsequent events. But, in general, dogs want to be with us. They love to love us. Our concerns are their concerns.

Dogs not only want to be with us, they want to please us. The more they want to please, the easier they are to train. Trainability, or obedience, is not a measure of intelligence or cognition: Wolves are far more intelligent than dogs. A wolf's brain is 150 centimeters larger than the brain of a comparably sized dog, but since they don't "want to please" man, wolves are much less obedient.

A wolf who has been raised by men since birth will never be as trainable as a domestic dog. While emotionally bonded to his human companions, and subordinate to them as a lower pack member would be, the wolf will always retain an autonomous spark of independence that commands respect.

We catch a glimpse of this long-submerged wolffian independence in the "intelligent disobedience" of the working guide dog. If a blind person gives the command "Forward," the dog will *only obey if it is safe for them to proceed.* His training has taken him beyond simply wanting to please his master by obeying a command to a higher level of under- standing. The guide dog accepts responsibility for his owner and trusts his own judgment over his master's command. Working guides "disobey" their owners regularly in this man- ner. Imagine the confidence and poise it requires for a dog— the product of thousands of years of bending to man's will— to summon his wolffian autonomy and work as a guide, or leader, without challenging his blind master's authority in other ways.

In creating domesticated dogs we have honed some wolf- fian instincts in our dogs, and we have dulled others to suit our needs. We kept much of the territorialism of wolves, and some of the suspicion of strangers, to make our dogs effective guards of our homes and property. We kept the wolf's ability to follow a creature's scent through the forest and even improved upon it when we created the various hunting dogs and the ultimate sniffing machine, the bloodhound.

Over thousands of years, through selective breeding, we've taken the rough-coated, prick-eared, long-nosed wolf and cre- ated dogs with sleek coats, floppy ears, and squashed noses to suit our fancy and our demands. We've sharpened and focused their passions until the Lab trembles with hunt antici- pation at the mere sight of a shotgun, and no self-respecting fox terrier can pass a hole in the ground (or a sofa) without checking it out for hidden foxes.

We've even used dogs to wreak havoc for us. The Spanish brought mastiffs from Europe to conquer the native peoples

in South America and the Caribbean, specially training them to disembowel Indians. During apartheid, South African paramilitary police crossed bloodhounds, Dobermans, and Rhodesian ridgebacks to produce a terrifying canine "track and attack" weapon.

We created dogs to suit our needs, and brought them with us as we've explored the globe. Their history is our own. What do we owe dogs for choosing life with us over the freedom of the wild? We owe them what they offer us—understanding, respect, loyalty, and love.

Serena rouses herself, stretches theatrically, and looks at me. "Shall we go out?" her expression asks. Why not? Time to take the wolf out for a walk.

Your Dog's Life

Courtesy of the author

I

Connecting with Your Canine Best Friend

Dogs are unlike any person or object we routinely interact with. Owning a canine means accepting responsibility for a member of a completely different species and learning enough about him—his needs, his drives, and how he thinks—to offer him an honorable life beside you.

You will need new skills and information in order to interact with your pet. Unfortunately, human instincts are not very useful when dealing with a canine. Thanks to the way some dog behaviors appear to us—your pet's look of slinking submission appearing to your eyes as a perfect impersonation of human "guilt," for example—your instincts about how to

treat your pet are as likely to be wrong as right. Human ignorance is how good dogs get ruined, why tragedies happen, and why we have shelters nationwide bursting at the seams with "owner-surrendered" pets.

The assumption that a dog will simply adapt himself to a human lifestyle is the greatest danger dogs face. We are very different species with significantly different ways of understanding the world. Humans communicate through the spoken word, but dogs primarily communicate through body language. We step outside and judge the day by whether it's sunny or cloudy. Like their wolffian forebears, dogs read the breeze, sorting through the information they get from the various smells. While our ears are stuck to our heads in one position, the canine's mobile ears swivel and prick up, focusing on distant sounds.

It is your job to learn as much as you can about your dog's perceptions. After all, your dog is not asking *you* to join *his world*. He was born into a canine pack. He could have stayed with his pack of origin. There he would have established his social ranking with his littermates and other pack members. His elders would have taught him manners and pack etiquette. Since the family spoke the same language, this learning process would be effortless. Other pack members would have spent all the time necessary to teach him pack rules, and would have enforced those rules consistently, in a language he understood. There would have been no miscommunication, and very little confusion along the way.

His day would have been full of group activities: waking up

together, finding something to eat, playing for a few hours, napping together, expressing affection by licking and grooming each other, and, finally, sleeping together, bodies touching, heads resting on others' backs. It is this instinct to do things with other pack members that genetically precodes him to want to do things with you.

Now imagine the confusion if the roles were reversed. Say you joined your pup's pack, rather than his joining yours. Since you don't speak "dog," communication would be intermittent at best. Some things you would understand: Expressions of affection, play, power, discipline, anxiety, reassurance, sadness, and joy all translate pretty easily (as they do in the other direction—from you to your dog). But if you ignored the lowered head, direct stare, and low growl of one of your packmates, which means "Come any closer to my bone, and you'll be sorry," and reached for the bone, you would get nipped. Hey, he warned you. Not in English, but in the common language of the pack.

In addition to the communication problem, you are also olfactorily and auditorially challenged, so you wouldn't be keyed into the scents, sounds, and other environmental cues of which the rest of the pack was aware. Uselessly squeamish about what you will touch with your nose or tongue, you wouldn't eat very well either. A pretty bleak outlook. You would have only one hope. If you were very lucky, a pack member might take pity on you, giving the extra time, patience, and energy needed to teach you to understand life in their world.

How lucky will your dog be in your pack?

By bringing a dog into your home you encourage him to bond with you and your family as his surrogate pack. You provide him with leadership, food, shelter, and emotional security in just the way his pack would. A domestic dog could learn to survive in nature if he needed to. The challenge is in helping him survive in *your world*.

This is what the dogs we own are up against—learning the ways of a foreign pack. His adjustment to your world will be as successful, or unsuccessful, as YOU make it.

What You Need to Know

Dogs have a completely canine consciousness and a canine identity. This canine consciousness means that your dog will expect you to act like a dog, will treat you and your family like other dogs, and will treat your home as though it were a doggie home until he learns differently. Training him is giving him the information he needs to join your life.

Because a dog will view your family as a pack, he will instinctively rank the members by leadership ability. You must be the leader in that hierarchy, with you and other family members ranking above your dog. This is particularly challenging with dominant dogs. They prefer to control things. Setting clear boundaries from the first day, and training your pet with obedience exercises, will help your dominant dog see you as the leader in the relationship.

Keep your dog in the center of her pack. Dogs hate isolation. Don't subject your pet to a life of watching its family from afar while tied to a doghouse, locked in a crate, or closed in the garage.

How Dogs Think

Canines think in a series of mental images made up of the stimuli the dog receives from his environment: what he sees but also what he hears, smells, tastes, and touches. Based on the dog's lifetime experiences, objects and events are remembered as either positive images ("I see the treat bowl on top of the refrigerator, mmmm, treats!") or negative images("Here comes my owner with a scowl on her face—the last time her face was like that I got hit. I'd better roll on my back to show submission, then maybe her face will smile").

Socialization is the process of giving our dogs positive mental images of the world in which they live: introducing our pets to unfamiliar people, places, sights, sounds, animals, objects, and activities in a nonthreatening manner.

Training your dog in a positive manner, using a happy voice and upbeat gestures, makes learning fun for your pet. Always offering praise and a reward to your dog for good behavior causes her to form positive mental images of herself obeying you.

She Can Read You Like a Book

Our dogs are profoundly tuned in to us. They take cues about how they should react to their environment from the emotions we project through our tone of voice as well as our body language. If we are tense and worried, our dogs match us with edgy, anxious behavior. They read not only our body language, but the different scents our bodies involuntarily give off, and their demeanor can be a revealing window on our own emotions. "It travels down the leash," I always like to say.

We willingly accept this idea when our dogs place a sympathetic paw on our knee as we sit glumly after some personal disappointment. Your dog did not overhear the upsetting conversation you had with your boss, or notice that a special person did not call, but he mirrors your sad mood with empathetic behavior.

We tend to forget that our dogs are always reading us, reproducing all of our moods. The feelings you project— happy, safe, unconcerned, worried, sad, or in danger—go from you and come right out of your dog. He learns about his environment by reading your reactions.

We can use the understanding of this connection to our advantage. If you use a happy voice and maintain a cheerful attitude during a stressful situation, your dog is likely to follow your lead (the way he acted sad when you were sad).

If you act the way you want your dog to act, he is likely to mirror your behavior.

A naturalist who was raising two wolves in her home described how anxious and distraught they would become after some small alarm (the doorbell, or a stranger walking past the house). She tried various ways to get the wolves to

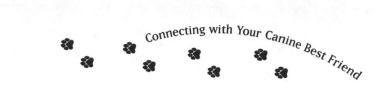

settle down, commanding them to be still, putting them in another room, distracting them with toys or treats, all to no avail. In fact, the more agitated she became in trying to *do things* to calm them down, the more agitated they became.

One day, following the postman's visit, the wolves were tearing around the house. This time, instead of becoming agitated herself and feeding their energy with commands and corrections the way she usually did, the researcher simply sat down on the couch, stretched in an elaborately relaxed way, yawned, and pretended to close her eyes for a nap. To her absolute amazement, the wolves immediately stopped their uproar and settled down near her. She peeked at her male wolf, and he had not only lain down, he was fanning the toes on his extended front legs in a stretch of his own.

If you can keep your cool and act cheerful, confident, and nonchalant when your dog becomes upset at something, you can not only deal with him more effectively because you are not upset, but your calm demeanor can defuse the situation. This is very hard to do because you have to harness your own emotions and behave differently than you genuinely feel inside. But if you can do it, it will really help you handle your dog.

Avoid the Punishment Trap

In an attempt to get their dogs to behave, dog owners frequently become fixated on "How can I punish him better?" or "How can I punish him in such a way that he understands what I want him to do?" However, dog ownership is *not* about punishment. It's about positively communicating with your pet in a way he understands and guiding him to prevent or avoid problems.

The wonderful American dog trainer/behaviorist George Quinlan and his wife, Sabilla, lead group dog-training classes together. At the first session, the dog owners and their families gather to discuss the aims of the course. George's goal is to get the dog owners to appreciate the awkward position their dogs are in because they live in a human home, and to show them how much guidance dogs need. To give his students a "dog's-eye view" of how confusing life with humans can be, he sets up a few demonstrations.

The first one highlights how unclear discipline and "punishment" can be to a dog. At some point in the evening, George has several chairs lined up next to a couch. He asks a member of the class to go and sit down. When the person sits on a chair, rather than on the couch, George bellows "NO!" at them. Usually the person jumps out of his skin in shock.

"Oh, I'm sorry," says George, "go ahead and sit down." If the person sits on a chair again, he wheels around and bellows at them. Sometimes it takes teenage boys three yells before they ask George, "Where do you want me to sit?" (interestingly, teenage girls usually ask George after the first bellow). "Sit on the couch," says George. "But you didn't tell me that, why are you yelling at me? This isn't fair," the person usually says, very rattled.

That is exactly George's point.

After apologizing, George explains to the class that a dog in

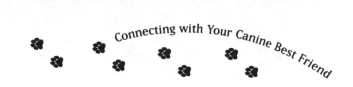
a human home has no way of knowing what the rules of the house are and what the owners want from him. Yelling at the dog or punishing him without giving him guidance is as unfair as George's yelling at the person for innocently sitting on the chair instead of on the couch.

Since you can't just sit your dog down and give him a forty-five-minute lecture outlining the "house rules," you have to find another way to communicate with your pet. I believe that dog owners need to let go of a focus on punishment and replace it with a focus on guidance. "What can I do to guide/supervise/distract/prevent this pet from doing what I don't want him to do?" and then reward him for doing the right thing so that he has a clear idea about which behavior is appropriate and which is not permitted in your home.

Many people resist this idea because it changes the responsibility for their dog's action from the dog to *them*. By vowing to guide and supervise to prevent the dog from doing something you don't want him to do, you are taking control of the situation. You are empowering yourself. Ironically, by focusing on punishing your dog after he has misbehaved, you make yourself a victim of your dog's behavior. Punishment happens only after an unpleasant incident. Guidance happens before.

When you need to correct your pet, use only measures that make sense to your dog: distraction to redirect his interest, a vocal correction, leash correction, or loss of social interaction (like putting a dog making mischief on a "down-stay" until he cools his jets).

You may think that hitting your dog, either with your hand or a rolled-up newspaper, is a good way to punish him. It is not. Dogs cannot rationalize punishment as humans can. There is no way to make your pet understand that "after he's taken his medicine" all will be forgiven. Dogs live in the moment; they have no conception of either guilt or redemption. All that your dog knows is that the person he has grown to love and trust is behaving violently with him. At best it will cause him to become wary and shy of you, and at worst it will prompt him to lash back.

How do you know if you're falling into the "punishment trap"? If your pet repeats a behavior you've already punished him for, he has proven to you that punishment doesn't work. By preventing him from doing the wrong thing again, you give him a chance to succeed instead of setting him up to fail. Punishment leads only to more punishment. Guidance and prevention lead to success.

To take preventive action, you need to be prepared with options. If you don't find all the preventive solutions you need to "answer" the problems your dog presents you with in this book (I'll cover as many as I can, but dogs can be very creative), don't stop here. Enlist the help of a trainer, even a behaviorist. They should offer you solutions to prevent your dog's problem behaviors. If they start to tell you "how to punish him better," go to someone else.

Don't fall into the punishment trap even if a "professional" tries to push you into it!

Canine Guilt

Dogs don't have a sense of guilt. "No way," you say, "my dog knows he's done wrong. He avoids me and looks guilty. He knows what I'm mad about when I hit him. He even acts happy after he's taken his punishment, because his conscience is clear." Folks, you're going to have to trust me on this, but your dog does not have a guilty conscience. He looks as if he's afraid of you because when you are furious you look very scary and your dog has learned to associate your angry expression with punishment—not because he "knows" he's done wrong.

If he relaxes after you've hit him, it's only because you have instantly relaxed.

The classic example is the owner who lets his poorly trained dog off the leash to run. When he calls the dog, it doesn't come promptly, and the owner becomes angry. The dog naturally reads the owner's displeasure (even from a distance, the body language and tone of fury carry!) and begins to avoid him, delaying the "come" even more. Finally, after much angry yelling, the dog slinks up to his furious owner and gets a slap for his trouble.

Yes, the dog should have come sooner. But the owner was a fool to let a dog who was not reliably trained off the leash, then give the dog a command that the owner could not enforce (had the dog still been on a thirty-foot leash, for instance, the owner could have snapped the line as a correction when the dog ignored his command, then reeled him in to lots of praise.

Let's Talk Dog

Sabilla Quinlan also does a remarkable demonstration at their introductory class. Unlike the "chair or couch" demonstration, her example shows owners how to communicate with their pets.

Sabilla, who speaks five languages, approaches a member of the class and begins speaking to the person in German. If he or she responds, she switches to French; this goes on until she finds a language the person does not understand.

Chattering happily in the foreign tongue, Sabilla beckons the person to follow her. Using smiles, nods of the head, gestures, and other nonlinguistic communication tools, she leads him around the room, has him sit down and stand up. When the person strays from what she wants, she frowns and shakes her head, then guides the person by beckoning and smiling encouragingly until the person does the desired action. She finds nonverbal ways to communicate what she wants the person to do.

This is a terrific exercise for the beginning dog owner to experience. You see firsthand how frustrating all our chatter must be to our dogs, and learn which nonverbal gestures, facial expressions, and sounds convey pleasure or displeasure. You also learn which gestures and sounds are the most effective tools for communicating with your pet.

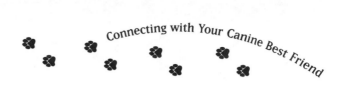

Practice Sabilla's communication exercise with another person. Using only gestures, expressions, and sounds—NO LANGUAGE— guide another person through two or three things. After practicing on a person, use these same skills on your pet.

Keep Things Simple

The human world you are making your dog inhabit is so strange to him that he must have easy, straightforward directions to begin to understand it.

Remember the experience of George and Sabilla's students? Imagine that you are lost in a foreign city. It is getting dark and you desperately need to understand the directions back to your hotel. An enthusiastic native is trying to help you. He has been talking fast and gesturing in different directions for a few minutes, but you can't understand anything he says. If he would just slow down, perhaps you could get something comprehensible out of him.

You stop him. Slowly and specifically you point up a street to the right and ask, "Yes???" He shakes his head vigorously, signaling "NO!" He points up a street to the left and says, "Yah, yah, yah!" This you understand. Five minutes later you are back at your hotel.

What does this have to do with communicating with your dog? When there is little common language, things must be broken down to the simplest state: right or left, good or bad, allowed or not allowed, "Good Boy" or "NO!" This is the direct level of communication you need to begin with to make

your dog understand how things work in the strange human world you've made him inhabit.

I'm not imposing silence on your household except for direct commands to your dog. But when you need to communicate something specific to your pet, like a command or a warning, *be succinct*. Extra talk will only confuse him.

Spend enough time teaching your dog what different commands mean so that there is no confusion. When you are sure he understands what you want from him, give him a command once. If he doesn't do it, the next thing out of your mouth should be a mild correction (a "No" and a clap of the hands, or a snap of the leash), then a restatement of the command "NO! Sit" to clarify. Anything else is just confusing noise.

Be equally as forthright with praise to reinforce the fact that he is doing the right thing!

Getting a Baseline Understanding of Your Pet

What do you know about your dog? Is she exquisitely sensitive to sound? Does she react to loud noises on the street or shrink from an angry outburst? In that case you've got a pretty easy communication tool at your disposal—your tone of voice! With a "happy voice" and an unconcerned air, you can reassure her that everything's okay when she becomes stressed. With a stern voice, you can easily communicate your displeasure, and you can guide her back to doing the right thing with a happy voice. A loud or deep voice (not shrill) will

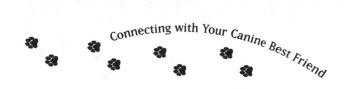
make you seem intimidating, while a soft, meek voice will be taken less seriously by a dog. This is one of the reasons dogs are more likely to view men rather than women or children as authority figures.

To get your dog's attention and make him want to join you, your tone should always be happy, upbeat, and positive when giving commands. Conversely, a correction should be delivered in a stern, dark tone of voice.

Does your pet live and breathe for her tennis ball? Then why not orient her learning around the joy she experiences playing ball—you've got a perfect reward for every positive behavior, a few minutes of ball play.

Would she sell her soul for a dog treat like my Serena would? It sounds like carefully using her food drive would "speak" best to her. You can even show her the treat to help her understand what you want her to do, then give it to her when she does it. For instance, following the treat in your hand down to the ground as you teach the "down" command helps your pet understand that "down" means putting her body in a lying-down position. When she achieves the position, she is rewarded with being allowed to actually eat the treat she has followed. When she has learned the command, you can replace the food reward with praise.

Instant Rewards Make Learning Fun

The easiest way to teach a dog something specific is to catch him doing it by chance, and reward him immediately. Keep a

pocket full of treats on hand to reward your dog for "chance" good behaviors. Eventually he will make the connection between your command and performing the task.

Everything your dog does and every interaction you have with him cause him to form a mental image and teaches him something. If you don't want him on the furniture, don't ever let him on it, even when he is little. It is much easier to do things right from the start than to fix things later.

With this in mind, you can constantly "work" your pet. Whether he is lying next to you as you watch TV (a down-stay), sitting next to you as you cook (sit-stay), or running toward you (come!), every single thing your dog does is a training opportunity. Simply add a command as he begins the activity, and a big reward at the end, and you've just had a training session.

Follow Through

Never give your pet a command you cannot enforce. This is one of the hardest things for people to do, because it runs contrary to human nature. We often impetuously command our dogs to do things when we have no way of giving them a correction if they don't comply. Because of this, we put ourselves in the position of becoming angry with a pet who is out of reach. Again, this gives the dog, not the owner, the position of control in the relationship dynamic. When we finally get the animal back, we let ourselves vent our anger on him—even if so much time has passed that the dog has forgotten the previous incident and has no idea why you are angry or why he is being beaten.

In the same way, you should always praise your pet when he does what you want. Have treats or a tennis ball in your pocket, and reward your deserving pet for good behavior.

Watch Out for Trouble

Don't let innocent-looking "dominant challenges" escalate. If you suspect that your pet wants to rule the roost (if you have an unneutered male of any of the "protection" breeds, your chances are excellent), be very tuned in to the little things he does.

Pushing past you to go out a door ahead of you, sleeping in your bed, sitting on the furniture at your same eye level (if he is giving you a "challenging look," not just sitting there with his eyes blissfully closed, being scratched), any kind of growl, or constantly demanding your attention are all signs of a leader-type dog who may someday challenge you. Be aware and be careful. This behavior starts innocently and can escalate with age and hormones. Good training and constantly reinforcing that you, not he, are the leader is the best approach.

What's Ahead

Dog ownership is essentially a relationship, subject to the same misunderstandings, joys, and sorrows as other relationships. There will be times when you absolutely don't get along, and times when it seems as though your dog has sprouted angel's wings.

In the following chapters, I'll guide you as your pet passes through the different developmental stages in the course of his lifetime. I'll outline his physical, mental, and emotional needs as he changes from frisky pup to stately gentleman. When your relationship with your pet begins to fray, I'll give you suggestions and tips to smooth out the edges.

It all begins with you learning about your pet, the little things that make your dog the individual he is. The more you know about that individual, the easier it will be to bond with him. Yesterday, a friend with a young dalmatian said, "It's amazing, every day she understands me better." "It's not just her," I answered, "it's you. Each day you know her better and communicate more clearly with her, so she can respond."

This understanding, this "knowing" of another sentient creature, is what dog ownership is all about. Enjoy!

2
Preparing for Your Pet . . .

> The possession of a dog today is a very different thing from the possession of a dog at the turn of the century, when one's dog was fed on mashed potato and brown gravy and lived in a doghouse with an arched portal. Today a dog is fed on scraped beef and Vitamin B_1 and lives in bed with you.
>
> —E. B. WHITE

Before your new dog comes home . . . you've got important work to do. A little preparation will give you a plan for managing your new pet, and the tools you'll need to make his transition to your home a success.

The Tools for Success

These items can be purchased at a local pet store or ordered from one of the many wholesale pet equipment catalogues like **Discount Master,** 800-346-0749; **R.C. Steele,** 800-872-7337; or **Doctor's Foster & Smith,** 800-334-3699.

You will need:

1. **A flat buckle collar to fit your dog,** with an identification tag that has your name, address, and phone number on it. Even if you haven't decided on a permanent name for your pet, order the ID tag, and put it on his collar immediately.

2. **A puppy gate or x-pen** (a collapsible dog pen) to contain your pet in a room or area. This is especially important for puppies during the housebreaking process.

3. **Either a thirty-foot cotton-web long line with a snap or a retractable flexi-leash** so that your dog will be able to run and play while still safely under your control. This is an important tool and will be crucial for teaching your dog to "come" when called.

4. **A regular six-foot or eight-foot leash.** I recommend nylon for a pup to get you through the two- to six-month "chewing" period, followed by leather when he starts to get strong. At that point, either nylon or chain will really hurt your hands.

5. **Extra newspapers, paper towels, disinfectant, and Nature's Miracle stain and odor remover** for the inevitable puppy puddles or the "mistakes" of an older dog who may take a few days to adjust to your home.

6. **An old blanket and pillow, or a dog bed,** so your new pet has a cozy spot to sleep in.

7. **Food and water dishes** that are hard to tip over. Nonchewable stainless steel or heavy crockery are the best.

8. Find out what **dog food** he has been eating from his breeder or previous owner and have a supply on hand.

9. **A few toys.** You can get more toys as you learn what kind your dog prefers, but have some on hand to give him appropriate things to chew on and play with.

What About a Crate?

Number ten on your list of things to have on hand when your new dog comes home is a crate. Most professionals use crates as a part of their dog's daily life. A crate under that kitchen table gives your pet a spot of his own without isolating him from your family.

Using a crate makes things much easier. Housebreaking puppies becomes very straightforward, and the omnivorous chewing machine that your teething puppy will become is kept safely away from your best shoes. Even older dogs appreciate a crate as a safe place to chill out. When dogs travel or stay at the veterinarian's, they are crated, so it makes sense to utilize one at home as well.

Small puppies accept the confinement of a crate easily. As long as you introduce your dog to a crate properly and never use it as "banishment," you can train him to use it at any age.

I recommend buying an "airline" type in which your dog can fly if he needs to (the airlines will make you buy one if you don't have your own). If you are buying a crate for a puppy, get the size that will suit him when he is a full-grown adult. Put a cardboard box or cinder blocks covered with a towel in the back of the crate, to take up extra space. Dogs usually won't go to the bathroom where they sleep, so your pup should have only a small space in the front, big enough for him to lie down and stand up, but not take several steps. If he has space to walk around in, he may go to the bathroom in the crate.

Decide where you plan to keep your dog's crate: either in your bedroom or in whichever room your family spends the most time during the day (the kitchen?), and set it up to your satisfaction before he arrives. I describe how to introduce your pet to his crate in the appendix.

Now the Plan

It really helps to have a strategy that the whole family is prepared to implement before your dog comes home.

First of all, decide who is going to be the "primary care-giver" for this dog. While the whole family should share in the care and training of your new pet, one person will need to oversee the operation. Your dog will build different relationships with different "pack" (family) members, but one person should have absolute authority over her. It will be easier for an adult to assume this role, since dogs instinctively respect an authority figure.

The important thing is to choose a person who will devote the necessary time and energy to caring for this pet every day, and who is assertive enough to thoroughly train her and give her the boundaries she needs to succeed in your home.

Where Will This Dog Sleep?

The next question, where this dog will sleep, is answered by where the primary caregiver sleeps. It is much easier for your new pet to understand that her new home is with you if she sleeps in the same room with you. The floor next to the bed of the primary caregiver, where she can see, smell, and hear her new owner, is the best choice for your pet.

Dogs always sleep with their pack, and the symbolic closeness of sleeping together is very important to them. If she's an older dog, sleeping in the bedroom of the new caregiver will help her to bond faster. If it's a puppy, it will calm his nerves as he faces his first scary night away from his brothers and sisters, and help him transfer his affection to you.

Put the crate or dog's bed in the bedroom, by the side of the bed where the nightstand would go. If you don't want your dog permanently in the bedroom, please begin with it there anyway. After a few weeks, when she is acclimated and secure, you can gradually move the crate, or dog bed, wherever you want it in the house.

A Safe Place to Play Outside

How will this dog go outside to relieve himself or play? Do you have a fenced-in yard where he can romp safely? Is there an enclosed area in a park or ball field nearby that you can use? If you don't have a fenced-in area for her to play in, YOU MUST NOT LET YOUR DOG OFF THE LEASH UNTIL SHE IS THOROUGHLY TRAINED. Even an older dog who is trained to come when called needs a period of adjustment to get used to *coming back to you, not her old owner.*

The answer to this problem is to use a thirty-foot line or flexi-type leash on your pet. On this line he can romp and play, even fetch sticks, but you remain in control and have the ability to bring him back to you.

Guide and service dog schools insist that the foster families who raise their puppies NEVER LET THE PUPS OFF THE LEASH EXCEPT IN FENCED-IN AREAS. No matter how well trained a dog is, you can never anticipate what distraction can cause her to bolt out under a car's wheels. These schools have lost enough valuable foster puppies in accidents to know that you can never be too careful. Your dog deserves no less.

Good Fences Make Safe Dogs

The very best way for your dog to play outside is to fence in a portion, or all, of your backyard. A high, dense fence will not only keep your dog in, it will keep out other wandering dogs, malicious neighborhood kids who might tease your pet, and wildlife.

However, if you plan to leave your dog outside when you are not home, the only safe way is in a locked, enclosed dog run with a fenced-in roof. Pet theft is rampant in this country, and unattended dogs are frequently stolen from backyards.

Even big and imposing dogs are not safe from pet theft; in fact, the larger the dog, the more they are worth on the "laboratory black market." My friend Martine found this out when her Great Dane, Katie, was stolen from her suburban Washington, D.C. yard. Thieves pass the dogs to "bunchers," who in turn sell them to licensed dealers, who then sell them to laboratories for testing. Thieves can make between $100 to $200 on each dog. By simply tossing an unsuspecting pet some meat, snapping a leash on him, and loading him into a van, these robbers can sweep through a neighborhood and make over a thousand dollars in an afternoon.

A fenced-in yard is the safest place for a dog, but leaving your pet outside alone for long periods of time is an invitation to trouble.

The Case *Against* Tying Dogs Outside

Many people choose to tie their dogs outside either on a run or a fixed chain. Aside from the danger of pet theft or the threat of a wild animal attack, leaving a dog tied outside has a profound psychological drawback.

A dog who is tied outside is constantly being provoked by

things in his environment that he is prevented from investigating. He is constantly being "teased" by everything beyond the length of his chain. This teasing acts as an agitating agent, and agitated dogs behave in overly excited, aggressive ways. Tying a dog and teasing, or "agitating," him is one of the ways in which attack-dog trainers bring out the aggressive drive in dogs.

This same scenario can occur in your backyard with a tied dog and children playing nearby. The dog wants to join them, but is prevented from doing so by the chain. He becomes frustrated and agitated, barking and whining. When the children come close enough, he is so revved up and stimulated that he immediately jumps on them enthusiastically, knocking them down or worse. Save your pet from this frustration by putting him outside only in a safely fenced-in area.

High-Tech Electric Fences

Electric "invisible fences" have become popular with home owners who choose not to fence in their property. These fences work by an invisible electrical current that runs around the property. The dog wears a collar that gives him a shock if he crosses the electrical current. Dogs quickly learn not to cross the invisible line, and under normal circumstances, stay in the yard. While these non-fences don't affect the appearance of your property, I *do not* consider them to be in the best interest of your dog.

A regular fence not only keeps your dog in his yard, it keeps potentially dangerous things *out* of your yard. Electric fences give your pet no protection from theft, wandering dogs, or wildlife. Your dog is at the mercy of whoever or whatever chooses to enter his property.

Also, while dogs generally stay inside the electric fence, they can easily become excited enough to run through the fence anyway, taking the shock. When a dog's prey drive is in full throttle after a squirrel or even a thrown ball, he is very likely to cross the fence and barely feel the jolt, since his adrenaline is running so high. But once outside the fence, the dog is trapped there! He knows very well that crossing his property line—in either direction—causes him to get a shock. After his adrenaline rush has subsided, he is faced with the unappealing option of taking another electric shock in order to return to his yard.

This frequently happened to a dog who lived a few houses from my parents. I would see him, tail tucked, slinking along the periphery of his yard, displaying classic approach-avoidance behavior. He was trying to screw up his courage to take the necessary shock to get back in his yard. I usually stopped, knocked on the door, and asked the owner to turn off the system and get his dog in the yard before the pet was hit by a car.

While "invisible" fences show off your yard, they are not the best solution for your dog. A conventional fence or dog run will give him room to exercise and protect him at the same time.

Preparing Your Home

Whether you are bringing home a puppy or a mature dog, your house needs to be prepared. Use this guide as you go from room to room making your home safe for your pet.

KITCHEN OR BATH

Put all cleaners, bleaches, and soap products in cabinets that cannot be opened with the nudge of a nose. You may need to install "baby-proof" locks. Potential puppy toys like brooms, dustpans, and mops should be put in shut closets as well.

Make sure you have a "dog-proof" trash can that cannot be tipped over and has a secure lid.

HALLWAYS AND FAMILY ROOMS

Put shoes, boots, and children's toys safely away in closed closets or chests. A lonely dog needs only five minutes of using a shoe or your child's favorite doll as a pacifier to ruin it. Store videotapes, books, and papers up high enough so that your dog can't grab them and tear them apart.

EVERYWHERE

Tuck any loose electrical wires under rugs or tape them up to the wall. Put houseplants out of reach. Tearing plants up by the roots and dragging them around the house can provide hours of entertainment for your dog, so get them out of his way. Most bulbs like narcissus, daffodil, and amaryllis, as well as some vines like wisteria and English

ivy, are poisonous to dogs, so put them far out of reach.

Finally, get down on all fours and make a "dog's-eye" tour of your home, just to check for any last "temptations."

In the Garage, Cellar, or Shed

Make sure tools, paint cans, chemicals, pesticides, rat poison, fertilizer, and plant food are stored high up, out of reach. This is especially true of ANTIFREEZE, which is a deadly poison to dogs. It smells and tastes sweet to them, so it is especially tempting, but licking up as little as a tablespoon can kill a dog. Lock it away.

In the Yard

If you have a fence, check it for holes, loose or splintered boards, or weak posts where your pet might escape. Hoses, lawn furniture with cushions, or anything else "chewable" should be put away.

I have known dogs who ingested everything from rat poison to wire-rimmed eyeglasses, so you can't be too careful. Please take this warning seriously, and save your pet from himself by "dog-proofing" your home.

Finding Your "Canine Support Staff"

You are going to need several canine professionals—veterinarians, trainers, and possibly a groomer for your new dog. If

you don't already have them lined up, start looking now so that you are prepared ahead of time. When you have settled on which professionals you are going to use, POST THEIR PHONE NUMBERS BY YOUR TELEPHONE FOR EMERGENCIES.

Also post this number by your phone:

NATIONAL ANIMAL POISON CONTROL CENTER, 800-548-2423

If your pet ever consumes anything suspicious, you want to be able to get help as quickly as possible.

Bringing Your New Dog Home

The best possible time to bring your new pet home is the first morning of a week- or two-week-long vacation. If that is impossible to arrange, the first morning of a weekend (try to make it a three-day weekend) is your next best bet.

The transition to your new home is a traumatic one, and you should be around as much as possible to bond with your new pet. Picking your new dog up early in the day gives him a chance to become accustomed to the sights, smells, and sounds of his new home. It also gives him time to get acclimated before bedtime, when you will expect him to settle down and sleep.

Even during these vacation days, you should leave your pet alone for an hour or so each day. He needs to become accustomed to being left alone, and to your coming and going. Introduce separation gradually instead of closing the door in his face the morning of your first day back to work.

With these guidelines you should have a plan, and the resources to make your new pet's transition to your home a happy one.

The Life Stages

Courtesy of the author

A dog's life span can be broken down into five stages: **puppyhood** (birth to eight months), **adolescence** (eight to eighteen months), **young adulthood** (eighteen months to three years), **adulthood** (three to eight years), and **old age** (nine years and older). I make these divisions to mark the changes

31

that occur as a dog evolves, and to guide owners as they address their dog's changing needs.

While dogs do pass through these specific stages, they don't leave one punctually and move on to the next. Changes are gradual, and there is much overlap. As hormones, life experiences, and physical and mental abilities change, one stage flows into another. An understanding of these stages will give you a guide to the issues your dog is likely to be dealing with as he matures. You should really visualize your dog's life span as one long transitional phase from birth to old age.

The age breakdowns above are based on the twelve-year average life span enjoyed by most medium-sized dogs. Small dogs generally live longer. A toy poodle, like my friend Suzy's dog Libby, might live to be fourteen or fifteen. I would expect Libby's life stages to break down to: adulthood, between three and eleven years; old age, eleven years on.

Large and giant dogs tend to have shorter life spans, sometimes only seven to nine years. A larger body simply works harder and gets tired out faster than a small and compact one does. Those giants will have much shorter life-stage periods: adulthood, three to six years; old age, seven and above. Consider what kind of dog you have and where her life stages/ages may fall.

The old "one dog year equals seven human years" is misleading. Dogs pass through periods of rapid development early in their lifetimes, and then age more gradually. It is helpful to imagine your dog at his relative human age in order to understand what emotions he may be experiencing.

A six-month-old dog is closer to a ten- or twelve-year-old child, while a year-old dog is more like a fifteen-year-old. The chart below will give you a feeling of these approximate ages.

Comparative Ages of Dogs and Humans

Dogs	Humans
3 months	5 years
6 months	10 years
12 months	15 years
18 months	20 years
2 years	24 years
4 years	32 years
6 years	40 years
8 years	48 years
10 years	56 years
12 years	64 years
14 years	72 years
16 years	80 years

A potential guide dog enters the world. A newborn Labrador retriever at Guiding Eyes for the Blind in Yorktown Heights, New York. *Courtesy of the author*

Guiding Eyes' Chessie lovingly bathes her new babies. *Courtesy of the author*

3
Before You Met Your Puppy . . .

. . . **h**e came into the world blind and deaf. His eyes and
ears were sealed shut, since his brain was still too undevel-
oped to understand signals from them. All that he had to
guide him to his mother's nourishing milk were his senses of
taste and touch. Since he had no ability to control his body
temperature, your pup was kept in a warm whelping nest
where he nursed and slept.

As the days passed, his brain, his body, and his consciousness developed. The twitching of his limbs while he dreamed
milky dreams helped his evolving muscles grow stronger and

more coordinated. The cells in his brain continued to multiply and connect.

The warmth of his mother's tongue as she lovingly bathed him, and the gentle handling of his human breeder, formed his emerging awareness of the comfort of touch. He will reexperience these first sensations of reassurance and contentment from humans and other dogs again and again during his life, every time he is licked or petted.

His mother fed, cleaned, and cared for him during this *neonatal stage* (birth to two weeks), but his breeder's involvement was also important. Petting and handling from birth teaches pups to accept and trust humans. Laboratory tests also show that early holding and exposure to stimulating sounds and objects cause pups to mature faster. These mild "stresses" produce an adaptive change in the pituitary-adrenal cortical system of a pup's developing brain, enabling him to deal with stress more effectively. Pups who have been handled by humans also perform better on problem-solving tests than pups who are left solely in the care of their mothers.

By fourteen days the world had begun to open up to the pup. He had entered the *transitional stage,* which begins with the opening of the pup's eyes. Although the eyes begin to open at two weeks, even short-range vision does not function completely until the pup is seven or eight weeks old. A pup's long-range vision is not accurate until he is three to four months old.

Your dog's most important sense—his ability to use his nose—matures very quickly. By five weeks of age puppies have an adult's ability to perceive scent. Why does scent develop much faster than vision or hearing? Stimulus from a dog's eyes and ears must work through the nervous system and cross to the opposite side of the brain to be decoded and understood. But scent information from the nostrils is converted directly into nervous impulses in the brain. Dogs can perceive scent only while they inhale, not as they exhale. You may notice your pup or dog pressing his nose to the bottom of a door and inhaling deeply. He is doing an "air exchange," literally sucking the smells from the other side of the door into his nose so that he can decipher who or what is on the other side.

As puppies develop perceptions beyond touch, they enter the *socialization stage.* By three and a half weeks pups are aware of the world around them and are beginning to form perceptions of that world. Suddenly a pup notices his littermates as more than warm lumps to snuggle with. His tail can wag, and he can bark at them! Slowly and clumsily pups begin to engage in play, toddling and rolling over each other like tiny sumo wrestlers.

All life experiences are "socialization." A dance begins between the genetic instincts a pup is born with and what he learns through experience about his environment. In every dog, inherited temperamental responses to stimuli are pitted against lessons absorbed from life. This dance, between nature and nurture, disposition and experience, inborn understanding and learned behavior, will continue for his entire life and will shape how he behaves. For the rest of his life, every

single experience will teach him something—forming either a positive or a negative mental image about the world.

Play-fighting with littermates is an important part of puppies' social development. It teaches them how to interact with other dogs and defines their status within the group. *Courtesy of the author*

This socialization stage can be broken into two phases. Weeks three to eight represent a pup's *litter socialization stage,* when his mother and siblings teach him "who he is" as a dog and how to get along with them. When he leaves his canine pack of origin and goes home with his new owner, a pup enters the second phase, the *human socialization stage.* At that time he learns his social position within his new human pack and the etiquette he needs to live in a human world.

Between the littermates and their mother, group, or "allelo-mimetic," activities become very important. Dogs make such wonderful human companions because they transfer their genetically precoded impulse to do things together to their human owners. The puppies sleep together, eat together, play as a group, investigate in a pack or in pairs, and even groom each other simultaneously.

Their play interactions become obvious little tests of confrontation, appeasement, dominance, submission, and cooperation. During these play episodes puppies learn crucial social skills: how to relate to each other and where as individuals they fit in with their pack. By the time they are seven weeks old, the leaders and followers within the litter will have been established.

These early lessons are essential to creating a healthy dog. Researchers have found that pups who are isolated from other dogs at this crucial stage become hyperaggressive to other dogs later in life. They also tend to be poorer learners, are less curious, are shyer, and exhibit a greater fear of other animals and noises. They are more likely to develop self-mutilative behaviors to channel their tension. In order to mature into confident, well-adjusted individuals, pups need a social education. Playing with their littermates is where they begin.

Within the litter the canine vocabulary dogs use to communicate is learned. Bowing down in front of another pup with your tail wagging in the air means "Come play with me!" A bark in the ear of a playmate and a quick circular dash means "Betcha can't get me!" The language for dominance and submission is also learned as the pups pin each other down, growl, and roll on their backs in play.

For the first two weeks of the litter socialization stage, pups will confidently approach any strange object, dog, or person. But after five weeks a *fear response* develops. Initially a pup recovers from a fright almost immediately. He is still innocent and trusting enough to regain his composure and reinvestigate the frightening thing. But as he ages, negative experiences begin to pile up and the fear response gets stronger.

The fear response is a survival skill. Nature uses it to teach young canines which things to avoid in their environment. If a pup undergoes a traumatic or painful event during this time, it can be very difficult to "undo" the lesson afterward.

At this same time they learn how to use their new teeth. Mother Nature gives puppies teeth that are sharper than their adult teeth will be. Very sharp teeth mean that even a little squeeze of the jaws hurts whoever is being bitten. The pups learn to squeeze less forcefully than they would if they had duller teeth. These training-wheel teeth teach pups to inhibit their bite so that when they are adults with tremendous jaw strength they won't use too much pressure.

A dog will go through this process of learning bite inhibition twice, once with his littermates and again when he goes to his new home. His human owners must teach him how much jaw pressure—none—is appropriate to inflict on human skin.

Sharp new teeth in a pup's mouth make nursing very painful for the mother and lead to the weaning process.

Weaning is the first conflict with a dominant leader that the pups experience. It changes the nature of their relationship with their mother. Until this point she has been a benevolent caretaker, but now, in order to force them to stop nursing, she must exert dominance over her pups, teaching them to do as she says.

How a bitch changes this relationship forms her pup's perception of what it means to be subordinate. This is critical because the subordinate position the pups must adopt with their mother mirrors the subordinate position they will assume with their human owner.

This is an important lesson. Without an idea of dominance and submission, a pup would be lost in dog society, where social rankings based on dominance knit the group together. More critically, pups raised without ever learning to be subordinate to their mothers rarely accept the leadership of a human owner and can be difficult or even impossible to train.

Ideally, a bitch gives her pups enough positive reinforcement during the weaning process for them to feel secure in their new subdominant position. A new learning bond is established between the mother and the pups.

A researcher at the Swedish Dog Training Center studied the interaction between German shepherd mother dogs and their pups during this critical period. He discovered that mothers weaned their pups—teaching them that they were no longer permitted to nurse—in different ways.

Especially tender mothers pawed their pups away from their sore nipples until the puppies got the point, rather than using a bite or a mouth threat. These mothers followed up with long, loving grooming sessions that restored their connection with their pups. In these cases, the mothers and puppies had exceptionally strong social bonds.

Most bitches used growls or bites to dominate their pups, keeping them from nursing. The pups rolled over on their backs, signaling submission to their mother. Reassuring grooming sessions followed to reward the pups.

But some mothers continued to aggressively dominate their pups even after the pups had moved away from the nipples. It was as though the bitches were punishing the pups for trying to nurse.

After these observations, the researcher tested the puppies. He found that pups from the punishing mothers were less socially outgoing and confident with people than other pups. They were less likely to freely approach a person, and when asked to retrieve a tennis ball, these pups were less able to participate. The aggressively dominating, punishing mothers produced pups too inhibited and confused about what was expected of them to perform confidently.

A mother dog punishing a pup even when he has withdrawn from her nipples is similar to a human owner who beats a dog to teach it, rather than showing it what is expected. With such a mother, or owner, a dog is left too confused to make a transition to a healthy subordinate relationship. If they can't understand what is being asked of them, they cannot obey.

Where did the dog mothers who were so punishing to their

How Do Wolves Do It?

Interestingly, the structure of a wolf pack makes these dominance lessons less traumatic for the pups. The mother wolf returns to hunting as soon as possible, leaving the pups with an adolescent baby-sitter. While most dog mothers are single moms, wolf pups have the benefit of both parents and the presence of other pack members. Researchers have witnessed even alpha male wolves puppy-sitting their young. This way the pups are spared the total shock of the mother-young conflict. Learning the lessons of dominance and submission from multiple sources gives wolf cubs a broader understanding of leadership and group hierarchy, preparing them for life within a pack.

pups learn to behave in that way? Female dogs learn how to treat puppies from the way they themselves were treated as pups. Like so many tragic human cases of children who were abused and then grow up to abuse their own children, parenting skills in canines are learned.

Hopefully your puppy's mother introduced the concept of dominance and submission in a positive, reassuring way. If she did, your job of setting boundaries for your puppy will be much easier.

Around six weeks of age puppies have their initial visit to

the veterinarian for an examination and inoculations. This event can leave a lasting negative impression. The pinch of an injection is usually the first time pups experience human-inflicted pain. This incident can cause a chain reaction of strong aversions in the pup.

From this simple episode a pup may acquire a lasting dread of veterinarians in general, the smell of the vet's office, and even the car ride. Many veterinarians are aware of the psychological importance of this first visit, and make a special effort to make the experience less traumatic.

Of course, if a pup's subsequent visit to the vet is less carefully planned, or very painful, negative associations can still be formed. Dogs learn experientially throughout their lives. But early negative episodes when the pup is the most impressionable make the greatest impression.

So by the time your puppy is eight or ten weeks old, when you are ready to meet him, he is ready for you. His brain is nearly developed, his body is coordinated enough to move about easily, and he has learned who he is compared with other dogs, as well as how to accept a position subordinate to your leadership. He is ready to begin the adventure of learning about the world as you socialize and train him to become your companion.

4
Eight Weeks to Eight Months
It's Puppy Time

> The "problem" of caring for a dog has been unnecessarily complicated. Take the matter of housebreaking. In the suburbia of those lovely post-Victorian days of which I write the question of housebreaking a puppy was met with the simple bold courage characteristic of our forefathers. You simply kept the house away from the puppy.
>
> —E. B. WHITE

Puppyhood is the magical time in your dog's life when he learns the most about the world. These months will be spent giving your pup the survival skills and manners he needs to live in your home.

What Is This Baby Capable Of?

Eight-week-olds are still infants. Mobile but clumsy, they will need to be taught to climb stairs and scale walls higher than their eye level. (Later on I'll talk about how you can use these interactions as confidence-building exercises.)

Your pup's body will change enormously in the next six months. At eight to ten weeks his bones are still soft and not even properly connected to each other. The size and weight of your pup's body may increase by four or five times in the first eight months of life. But don't let increasing size fool you. Depending on the breed and size of the dog, it can take up to two years for his bones to finish growing. Some large breeds have not really finished "muscling up" until three or four years of age.

Courtesy of the author

For this reason you should not encourage your pup to do too much strenuous running, jumping, or roughhousing until his body is fully grown. Stressing immature bone and tissue can lead to injuries. Let your pet play and blow off steam, but don't force him into too much activity too soon.

You can expect your puppy to be forgetful and to require repetition in his training. A dog's brain does not begin to function at an adult level until at least six months of age. Females and smaller breeds tend to mature more swiftly. (I have known many male pups whose lightbulb didn't go on until they were a year old!) He may master a command quickly one day, but look at you blankly the following day when you give him the same command. Patiently repeat lessons, from housebreaking to "sit," until your puppy is old enough to retain them. You will notice a startling improvement in his retentive ability when he is closer to a year old.

A canine's long-range vision does not mature entirely until about four months of age. Before that time, your puppy may see fuzzy or indistinct shapes. This blurry vision can cause him to bark at people or objects—even if he has seen them before. Never assume that your puppy can see you. Always speak to the pup to identify yourself, and reassure him if he has a startled response.

Noises, sights, smells—your new pup has a huge job sorting through, identifying, and cataloguing the world around him. Be sensitive to this process and help your pup "organize" his environment by giving him a routine. Accelerate the cataloguing process by introducing him to different stimuli through socialization, as I describe in the appendix.

Emotionally, pups develop in stages. Your dog may be confident and bold one week, reticent the next. When your pup is between six and ten weeks of age, you may notice that he has a greater fear response. During this period pups are less confident and more easily traumatized than is their nature. Nature uses this time to teach young dogs what to avoid in their environment. Research suggests that many pups pass through a second "fear imprint" stage between four to six months of age.

Take special care to protect your puppy from frightening episodes during these fear imprint stages. If he has a trauma, make an effort to reintroduce the frightening thing in a gentle, positive way to help him overcome his fear.

The first four weeks with your pup are a love affair. He is your little shadow, responsive and eager to please. This is the best opportunity to set the ground rules for your life together. It won't be this easy again for a year or two. All the basic commands described in the appendix can be introduced during this time, although you should not expect your pup to learn them. If you introduce them early and reinforce them consistently, he will learn naturally.

Around twelve weeks even the "clingiest" pup becomes more independent. They discover that you are not the only interesting thing in the world and are less likely to blindly follow your lead. This process is part of your dog's developing individuality, but presents obvious safety problems. To supervise and guide your pup through this period you must keep him on a thirty-foot leash. Allow him to build exploratory self-assurance, but always be able to call him back to you or pull him out of harm's way.

As the weeks pass, your puppy's energy and exploration level will increase. Be prepared for these changes by using

these guidelines to start off on the right foot and get you through the trying times.

The First Day Together

When you arrive home with your pup, put her flat buckle collar on her and snap on the leash. Before you take her in the house, put her down on the ground to sniff around and go to the bathroom if she needs to.

Inside the house, accompany her as she investigates her new surroundings. Don't let her tear off on her own; she may be looking for a spot to relieve herself. After a few minutes, you should do formal introductions. Get all the human members of the family together, and have everyone sit in a circle. If there are only two people in the family, sit about five feet apart, facing each other.

The first person who brought the pup into the room should bring her into his lap, pet her, say her name, and make eye contact with her. After a few moments, pass the leash to the person opposite. That person should call the puppy, using her name and the "come" command. When she turns in the direction of her name, she should be coaxed and gently guided to the lap of that person. During this process, she is petted and praised, and has the chance to make a scent imprint of her new family.

Your puppy should go around the entire family twice— back and forth two or three times if there are two of you. The whole process should last only ten minutes. Keep the mood calm and happy. Help children keep their voices low and have

them stroke the puppy's fur without grabbing skin or pulling the ears and the tail. Be sure that they remain seated when handling the pup to prevent them from dropping him.

You can practice this same exercise several times a week to help your puppy learn the "come" command.

When we brought Fergus home we did the whole "sitting in a circle" introductions thing. He was so small, just a tiny little guy, but he went bravely to everyone in the family. It was as though he was saying, "Now I belong with you."

—PHILIP, OWNER OF WEST HIGHLAND TERRIER FERGUS

Let's Talk Housebreaking

You need to be prepared for housebreaking from the outset. Without a plan in place your pup can quickly fall into bad habits that can be difficult to change.

A young puppy's digestive system is so small that it needs to evacuate frequently—as often as every two hours. As they get older, the period of time between bathroom visits lengthens. But if your pup is left alone for a six- or eight-hour workday, you should expect him to need papers on the floor until he is perhaps six or eight months old. Only then will his system be strong enough to wait a whole day until you return home.

I know that this may sound like a long time to be involved with housebreaking. However, puppies, like little children, are

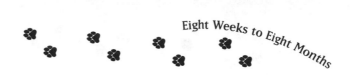

not very self-aware. They often do things without thinking. To be housebroken, your pup must learn to think first before doing his business, and either wait until he goes outside or signal to you that he needs to be let out to relieve himself. How quickly your pup grasps these concepts will depend on how consistently and clearly you present the process of housebreaking to him, and how mature he is.

If you teach your pup in a straightforward, unemotional manner, then he will soon understand what you want of him. But if you give confusing signals, become hysterical at a mess, or frighten him with senseless "discipline" like beating him or sticking his nose in it, you will only make the process more difficult. Don't undermine your own objectives by reacting in anger.

How I Housebreak My Pups—The Supervision Method

Dogs have a natural revulsion to sleeping near their own waste. Housebreaking your dog is simply channeling this natural instinct: teaching your pup that the taboo of evacuating in his nest extends to your entire house.

Dogs prefer to do their business on "natural" footings, like grass, and you can use this preference to your advantage. It will help your pup understand that outside is correct, inside is prohibited. By praising him for going outside, you will teach him to associate being outside with evacuating.

This supervision method is by far the simplest and makes the most sense to a dog because it is consistent with his instinct to keep a clean nest. But it does require you to carefully monitor your pup's actions.

As part of the supervision method we have always used voice commands to cue our dogs to evacuate. I learned this approach working with guide dog puppies, who must be trained to evacuate on command. Of course, if a dog doesn't have to "go," giving him a command won't make any difference. But if he does, the command jogs his memory and reminds him to get on with it. We use the command "Get busy," but you can use any command you want. British guide schools use the phrase "Do your little job" (there will *always* be an England), but any short command will do.

Instituting the Supervision Method

1: **Keep your pup with you when you are in the house.** Use an umbilical leash so that you can supervise his actions. If he is not being monitored, he should be in puppy central, as I describe on page 54, with papers down on the floor for his use.

2: **Take him outside as a matter of course every two hours, or as often as you can. Encourage him to evacuate by using a command like "Get busy."** If he doesn't go after a few minutes of encouragement, bring him back inside and try again in thirty to forty minutes.

3: **Control what goes into your pup as well as what comes out.** Giving your pup three meals each day at regular intervals as I describe on page 185 will give his digestive system a schedule you can depend on. Don't make the mistake of leaving food available to your pup at all times. Be sure that your puppy's last meal is early in the evening, giving him plenty of time to evacuate before settling down for the night.

4: **Watch him during "prime times."** After a nap, a meal, or a long playtime, pups usually go to the bathroom. The minute you see him "looking for a spot"—searching around in a preoccupied way—grab him. Don't take the time to call him to you. Just scoop him up in your arms in an upbeat manner, saying, "No, no, outside!"

5: **Take him straight outside.** Hold him off the ground until you get to an appropriate spot. Put him down and give the command "Get busy!" The excitement of being outside may distract him for a moment, so give him a few minutes. Don't engage him in play—that would distract him even further—just keep encouraging him to "get busy." When he finally does go, praise him with "Good boy, get busy" to reinforce the command with the action.

6: **Your pup may need to go outside during the night.** If she whines to go out, accommodate her, but don't play with her or give her any food. When her business is done, praise her and return her straight to bed. My eight-week-old pups often wake me around three A.M. for the first week, but soon sleep through the night.

WHEN ACCIDENTS HAPPEN

If you catch your pup in the act, say "no" and carry him outside to finish with lots of praise. If you completely miss the deed and find an old mess, don't make a fuss about it. Your pup will have only a vague memory of it—ancient history in his puppy's brain. Any attempt to discipline him after the fact will only confuse your pup. Clean it up when he's not around, and put Odormute or Nature's Miracle on the spot. If you don't clean it up thoroughly, the lingering scent may tempt him to reuse the location in the future.

So put down that rolled-up newspaper! Sticking your puppy's nose in a mess is another useless form of discipline. It is *not* a revolting or unpleasant experience for your dog—as it would be for you. Though repulsive to us, coprophagy—the eating of feces—is a common canine behavior. If anything, sticking your pup's nose in his mess might make him think that you *want* him to eat it. If you do not want your dog to acquire this disgusting habit, don't suggest it to him.

Puppy Central and the Umbilical Leash

Like a toddler on the loose, your puppy can *only* get himself in trouble if you give him the unsupervised run of the house. Instead, you need to build a "puppy central" in your home and plan to use an umbilical leash.

Puppy central is an area where your dog will be safe and confined when you are not at home, or where he can take a "time out" when you can't manage him underfoot. Puppy central gives him a place to chill out where he can still hear and see you. Just being able to stretch out and snooze in a quiet spot close to his master is a pleasure to a dog. A crate can serve this same purpose, functioning as a secure spot close to humans where a dog can have his own space. Puppy central should be just that—central to your life—not closed away in a cellar or upstairs bedroom.

An exercise pen with papers on the floor, toys, and available water makes an excellent "puppy central" in your home. *Courtesy of the author*

Select a corner of the kitchen or a centrally located bathroom or hallway for your puppy central. Make sure the floor of this area is covered with linoleum, tile, or some other waterproof surface. Using puppy gates, furniture, or a portable, collapsible wire pen called an x-pen, partition off an area large enough for the pup to move around freely. Cover the floor with papers, add a water dish, chew toys, and an old towel for snuggling. Ideally, move your pup's crate into "puppy central" for daytime use, and back to the side of your bed for the night.

I have found an umbilical leash to be very effective. When working around your house and yard, simply attach a leash to your puppy's flat buckle collar, slip the loop-handle end through a belt, and buckle the belt around your waist. Your pup is now attached to you, but your hands are free.

With the umbilical leash you can go about your business with your pup at your side. You should encourage your pup to move or sit with you, but otherwise ignore her. This teaches her to focus on you. When you move, she moves; when you stop, she is encouraged to sit; when you sit down, she lies next to you. She is supervised and under control, but is not the center of your attention.

USING THE CRATE

Many professionals crate-train and housebreak their pups simultaneously. A normal pup will not mess where he sleeps. If you accustom him to spending an hour or two in his crate, you don't have to worry about him soiling the house during that time.

I describe how to train your pup or dog to use a crate in the appendix. Refer to those instructions as you introduce your pup to his crate.

In addition to these supervision methods, you may choose

to block off the living room or dining room with well-placed dog gates. Make sure that these are securely in place and can't be pulled over or crashed through by an enthusiastic pup.

With these options you should be able to housebreak your pup. If you continue to have problems, consult a trainer. Usually, simple advice can get things straightened out quickly.

When we brought Haley home from her breeder, I thought I was prepared for the housebreaking thing, but it was much crazier than I expected. Things just happened so fast. I mean, I would take her outside and she would go, then five minutes later we would be back in the house, playing, and she would squat again. There was no time to put on my coat or anything, I just had to grab her and run back outside. This went on for the first two weeks. When we weren't home we used the bathroom as puppy central, and that worked fine. But when we were home with Haley, it was really hard. Half the time she sneaked behind the sofa, or she did it when my back was turned. I thought I would lose my mind chasing her around the house to take her out after she had already gone. I was so fed up. Finally I started using the umbilical leash and it really turned things around. Haley couldn't sneak off to go in a corner, and since I didn't have to chase her, I was much better about taking her out regularly. By the end of the first week of using the umbilical leash, she started whining to tell me she needed to go outside, and from that point on we were fine.

—ALLISON, OWNER OF COCKER SPANIEL PUP HALEY

A Daily Plan

Your new puppy's days will be spent playing, exploring, evac-uating, eating, and sleeping. We have always fed our puppies three small meals a day until they are a year old, then cut back to two daily feedings for their adult lives.

Let's talk specifically about daily life with this pup. During the first six to eight months, your pup's routine should look something like this:

7:00 A.M. Let your pup out of her crate next to the bed and imme-diately take her outside to relieve herself. After your morning chores are done, feed your pup breakfast and then take her out again for a brief romp or walk.

8:15 A.M. As your family goes off to school or work, close your puppy in puppy central, the kitchen, or the bathroom, with a puppy gate preventing her from gaining access to the rest of the house. Leave water and toys available to her and cover the floor with papers.

12:30 P.M. A family member or neighbor should stop by to let your pup out to go to the bathroom. She should be fed a small lunch, and taken outside again before returning to puppy central for the afternoon.

5:30 P.M. Once the family is home, your pup should be taken out-side for a good, long romp or a walk and a training ses-sion. Back inside, she should be fed her supper, taken outside briefly to eliminate, then settle down with your family for the evening.

Evening   Give your pup a "body handling" session, when family members "groom" or massage the pup and then play with her.

Bedtime   Your pup is taken outside for last time, and then, when the family goes to bed, is returned to her crate for the night.

APPROPRIATE CORRECTIONS AND REDIRECTION

Since your pup is especially vulnerable to traumas, you need to be aware of the discipline you give him. Always keep corrections clear, quick, and precise. The instant your pup stops doing what you were correcting him for, immediately redirect his attention to something positive.

You can interrupt your pup, correcting him from misbehaving by:

- A sudden clap of the hands and a loud "no" followed by distraction and praise.

- Growling "No!" and picking the pup up (without shaking him) so that his feet are just off the ground. Suspending him in the air stops whatever mischief he was up to. Hold him off the ground for a moment while you growl, then put him down and distract him with a toy to redirect his interest.

- A snap of the leash if he is on the umbilical leash.

Expect to repeat lessons and corrections over and over with your puppy. Gentle yet firm guidance is what he needs.

Starting Off Right—Rules and Boundaries

From the very first day, think about how you want your dog—not your pup—to behave.

If you don't want a mature dog who sleeps on the couch, crashes through a doorway to go outside, enthusiastically jumps up on people, barks a lot, or nips, don't let him do those things as a pup. Within a few months he may weigh eighty pounds, but he will see life through his same puppy eyes. He won't understand that jumping up for kisses, which was cute before, has become life-threatening to you because of his size. Letting him "get away" with naughty behaviors because he is cute invites problems down the road. It is also unfair to your dog. Don't change the rules on him halfway through the game; be consistent from day one.

Here is my list of behaviors that even the youngest pup should be forbidden to do:

No jumping up: Jumping up is a challenge, since dogs greet and show respect to their elders by licking the face and mouth of the senior individual. This is why pups try to lick our faces, and will jump and claw their way up to do it. They are telling us in dog language that they love and respect us.

As flattering as this may seem, it won't work in your world.

Eight-week-old Tucker shows respect, affection, and submission to her thirteen-year-old great-grandmother Moni by licking Moni's face and mouth. Your pup may try to express those same emotions to you by giving you "kisses." *Courtesy of the author*

Teach your puppy instead to greet you and show respect by sitting in front of you (refer to teaching the "sit" command in the appendix). You can have your pup sit between your knees while you crouch down over her, even lean in and let her lick your face, or give her a hug as long as she stays sitting.

No mouthing, or play-biting humans: Dogs express emotions like dominance or reassurance by mouthing each other and explore much of the world with their mouths. Puppies, like toddlers, put everything in their mouths, from crayons to slippers. It is natural exploratory behavior. However, your puppy must learn that mouthing humans is not allowed.

If your pet seizes any part of your flesh with his teeth, you should react! Yell in pain and make a big show of how hurt you are while saying, "No bite." The shock of your extreme reaction should teach him the consequences of his actions. Offer him a toy to play with as an appropriate alternative, or encourage him to lick you with the command "Kiss."

If your show of pain doesn't stop him, grab the skin on either side of his face as you say "No!" very forcefully. He should freeze for an instant. Let him go and offer him a toy to play with instead. Simply pushing your puppy's mouth away when he bites you will establish a fun bite-and-shove game that he will want to play more.

Many people unwittingly encourage their pups to bite by teasing them: softly slapping the dog on the face or wagging a finger in front of his nose. Be sure no member of your family is "playing" with your pup in this way.

No rushing out through doorways: Controlling the entry and exit to your home is a sign of your leadership position and can save your pup's life. Keep your youngster on the leash and begin practicing his "sit" and "stay" commands (described in the appendix) at the doorway. Give your pup a release command such as "okay" to let him pass through the doorway. Learning to wait for your release command will keep your pup safe and under your control.

No jumping on the furniture: Make your pup sit or lie on the floor next to you. He can even press his body into your knees if he wants to be closer to you, but he cannot get up next to you. Allowing your pet to be on your same eye level can lead to dominance problems as your dog matures.

Positive Things to Do with Your Pup

The last section focused on "don'ts," but what about the "do's"? Do start training her right away with the obedience exercises. Work on confidence-building exercises and play together. Teaching your pup to retrieve or use her nose to find treats will establish a healthy pattern of working together.

In the appendix I describe exactly how to teach basic commands to your pup or older dog. Begin with "watch me" and "sit." Introduce walking on a leash by using the umbilical leash technique around the house and taking your puppy out for walks around the block to reinforce the idea of "going places together."

Start "come" work right away, but be careful not to let your puppy off her thirty-foot line. It is unlikely that any dog under eight or nine months can be trusted entirely to "come" when called—they just aren't mature enough. So don't tempt fate.

Enroll your puppy in a local puppy kindergarten class where these commands will be introduced. Puppy class is the one hour a week when the spotlight is on your puppy. She has your undivided attention and is in a fun, interesting environment surrounded by other puppies. While she is having fun,

A Daily Massage Routine

Have your pup sit in front of you and run your hands over his entire body while you talk softly to him. "Inspect" his ears, teeth, elbows, stomach, and each leg, paw, and individual toe. Accustom him to the feel of metal touching his toenails by touching each nail with a metal spoon or fork—this will prepare him for the toenail clippers. Do all of this gently, as you speak softly, offering a treat every few minutes so that he enjoys the touching.

Use long strokes down his back in the direction of his hair to get him to relax, then work on individual parts. As you go over his body gently, begin to massage his muscles with your fingers. You can use stroking motions or small circles. Your pup will soon relax into your touch, his eyes closed in blissful reverie. He may even flop over on his back to give you full access to his body. End by rubbing his ears where they connect to his head.

If your pup does not enjoy his massage, be sure you are not kneading his skin too strongly. Don't force him to hold still if he really starts to panic; let him go and act jolly to relieve his fears. Give him a treat, then do something else with him to take his mind off the incident. Try a little more "touching" an hour or so later.

you are learning to handle her and are working with a professional who can give you advice as she matures.

Always have your pet perform or work (a simple "sit" is a performance) to earn petting. This approach positively reinforces your pup's training by giving her so much practice. It also establishes you as your pup's leader. Don't let your baby get the idea that you exist to serve her. You must be her boss, and asking her to do a "sit" or a "down" command in order to earn praise reinforces your leadership in her eyes. Establishing yourself as the leader during puppyhood is as important as housebreaking!

Confidence-Building Exercises

Confidence building is simply encouraging your pup to do things to build her trust in you. This can be something as simple as climbing stairs—a daunting task for a little puppy. Get them to crawl under, climb over, and walk the length of the same fallen tree, or to cross a stream. By encouraging and guiding your puppy through such episodes you are teaching her to have faith in you.

Confidence-building exercises are wonderful for all pups, especially shy or bold ones. Succeeding at the exercises, and receiving your praise, gives a shy pup confidence. Working high-energy bold puppies over obstacles will get them to focus on you instead of just charging into life with you in tow.

So work your pup. Practice going up and down different types of stairs—even try cellar stairs with air between the steps.

Nose Work

Your young pup may not be as athletic or obedient as she will become, but one thing she does have at this age is a first-rate nose. I suggest starting "nose work"—games and exercises to get her using her sniffer—right away, as early as eight weeks of age.

Begin by playing simple games of "Find It!" with your pup. Start with a juicy piece of hot dog or cheese (these have a stronger smell than dry treats). Have your pup on the leash and sitting down. Tell her "Wait" and hold the leash so that she can't get up until you let her. Show her the treat and place it on the ground an arm's length in front of her. As she sees the treat placed, give her the command "Okay, find it!" with a happy voice to release her from the sit, encouraging her to go for the treat. Give her lots of praise as she gobbles down the snack.

Always make her sit and "wait" first as you gradually place the treat farther and farther away from her. Give her the command "Okay, find it!" and the direction in which to go to start the game, and always first let her see where you put the treat. She should soon be taking several steps to "find" her reward.

When she can reliably "find" her snack all the

way across a room, you can start placing it while her back is turned. This is when you will start to see her really use her nose. Always give her the correct direction to go in, and help her to find her treat by indicating where it is—this teaches your pup to look to you for guidance. Gradually you can work up to hiding the treat out of her view and hiding multiple treats in a room or yard. Remember, the point is for your pup to succeed and start using her nose, not for you to hide the treat in such a way that she will fail. Keep the games short, fun, and, most of all, successful for your pup.

An eight-week-old Lab pup already using her nose in a game of "find it." *Courtesy of the author*

Use fallen trees as I described. Ideally, visit a children's playground and take your puppy up and down the stairs, across the bridges, and even down a gentle slide. Never force a frightened pup, and always be at your pup's side with encouragement, physical support, if necessary, and a treat reward.

By the time our golden, Buddy, was four months old, he was a nonstop motion machine. He was so high energy that I couldn't deal with him. We got him in puppy class, but he just dragged me around trying to play with the other pups. The instructor was patient, but Buddy was really disruptive. I was embarrassed and angry. Most of all, I couldn't believe I was in a fight with my own dog. Finally, at the fourth puppy class, some people from a local agility club brought a few obstacles for our puppies to work with. For the first time, Buddy found something he liked to do but that required him to slow down and concentrate. By the end of the class, I realized that we had worked together as a team for the first time. I started taking Buddy to the playground in the evenings and working him over the kid's jungle gym. It got him tired out and focused on me enough for us to be able to practice other commands as well.

—MARILYN AND HER GOLDEN RETRIEVER, BUDDY

Puppy Socialization

Many veterinarians recommend that puppies not be taken to public areas until they have been fully vaccinated—as late as

fourteen weeks of age. This is based on a medical concern that your pup could become infected with a canine illness like distemper or parvovirus by touching noses with, or sniffing the feces of, a sick dog.

While the risk of infection is a concern, you *cannot* let it stop you from beginning to socialize your pup. If you do as the vets suggest, you will have missed a critical socialization time and may never be able to make up the exposure. This eight- to sixteen-week sensitive period is a once-in-a-lifetime chance to mold your dog. You cannot afford to lose it.

I suggest getting your puppy out from eight weeks on, but using *extreme caution*. Find healthy dogs in your neighborhood and arrange for them to come to your house to visit your pup once or twice a week. Since these dogs are fully vaccinated, there will be no risk of infection. If a strange dog off a leash comes along when you have your pup out in a park or a mall, pick your puppy up off the ground to prevent her from touching noses with the stranger. Don't let your pup sniff old piles of feces left by other dogs. Do everything you can to expose your puppy to the wide world, but don't risk exposing her to infection until her immunizations are finished.

What should your pup be socialized to? Think of the various components of your human life that will be unfamiliar to a dog. Each one will need to be introduced gently and positively to your pup until it is as familiar to her as it is to you. I describe ways to socialize your puppy in the appendix.

Weekends offer a wonderful chance for puppy socialization

time. Whether it's a Little League game, a neighborhood barbecue, a skating party, or a trip to visit family, bringing your young canine with you will broaden her horizons.

Visiting the Veterinarian

Puppies receive such frequent vaccinations in the first four months that they can develop a real fear of the veterinarian. To counteract this, I suggest that you make a point of stopping by your veterinarian's office between visits. The staff and your vet can give your pup a few treats and a moment of petting. These "treat visits" will make your pup more comfortable during her real visits and may help her avoid a lasting mistrust of veterinarians.

Body Handling

Dogs need to be accustomed to having their bodies touched. At the doctor's office or at home they need to learn to accept the restraint and manipulation of handling. Use the routine on page 64 to introduce your pup to gentle handling.

Another fun way to practice body handling is to "dress" your pup. Start with an oversized T-shirt. Have your puppy sit in front of you and put the T-shirt over her head. Lift each front leg and draw it through a sleeve. Pull the body of the shirt down over your pup's back. Have this "dressed-up" pup walk around the house with you, then remove the garments in the same way. When she can sport her T-shirt with ease, add socks on all four feet!

Teething

Since teething is a part of puppyhood, so is chewing. It is normal for pups to want to chew on objects. It makes their sore gums feel better. For most pups, the chewing of teething is a transitory stage. When the permanent teeth are in place, few dogs chew excessively, but during the process, watch out! Several ice cube treats a day will help soothe the pain of your pup's sore gums. Be sure to give your pup plenty of appropriate toys and bones to be chewed on during this time, and keep "chewables" you don't want destroyed, like shoes and children's toys, put safely away in closed closets.

The Puppy "Crazies"

One unforgettable aspect of puppyhood is a sudden attack of the "crazies." The scenario goes something like this: Your pup wakes up from a nap or finishes his dinner and suddenly gets a crazed look in his eyes. Before you know it, a furry tornado is zooming around your house. He dashes from room to room, grabbing toys as he flies by. He jumps on the couch, runs under the table, rolls across the rug, barks at the window, and is off again. As suddenly as the attack began, it is over. He comes trotting up to you panting, tail wagging, very pleased with his display.

What just happened? A fit of joie de vivre, perhaps? Pups go through play attacks in the same way kittens will suddenly throw themselves at a spool of yarn, or a foal will kick up his heels and race across a pasture. They are simply happy to be alive and are letting off a little steam. Enjoy these episodes, as startling as they may be. When your pup is a stately gentleman, you may miss the silliness of the "crazies."

To Spay or Neuter?

The end of puppyhood is marked by your dog entering puberty. During puppyhood your pup has matured sexually as well as physically, mentally, and emotionally. I firmly believe that all companion pet dogs should be spayed or neutered. Hormonal changes make your jolly pup more temperamental and unspayed/unneutered dogs suffer from hormonally linked cancers like prostate and breast cancer. There is no question that spaying or neutering helps prevents medical and behavioral problems. Ben Hart's studies at the University of California showed startling changes as a result of neutering male dogs: Roaming was reduced in 90 percent of the cases; inter-male aggression was reduced in 60 percent; mounting behaviors (on people) was reduced in 60 percent; and urine marking in the house was reduced in 50 percent. Neutering will not affect his working ability. It will tone down a bossy pup, making him more willing to accept your leadership.

The ideal time to spay/neuter a dog depends on the individual's size and temperament. The operation is the easiest and most effective if done well before the onset of puberty, which is signaled by a female's first heat, or dominant leg-lifting behavior in a male pup. For male pups, this may mean as early as four to six months of age. Females are usually spayed around six months, just before their first heat cycle.

The idea that each dog should experience sex in his or her lifetime, or bear a litter, is an example of humans projecting their own desires on to dogs. Remember that the submissive wolves who accept a place in the pack below the alphas are not sexual at all. Stack the deck in your favor—spaying or neutering your pup will help him to be the companion pet you want to share your life with.

Enjoy your dogs' puppyhood. They grow up very fast. *Courtesy of Ruth Anderson*

Let's Recap:
THE FIRST EIGHT MONTHS—WHAT TO EXPECT AS YOUR PUP GROWS UP

8–10 weeks

- Your new pup should have learned her name, become acquainted with all the members of the family, and your schedule and system for dealing with housebreaking should be well in place.

- Around the house, you should be using the umbilical leash on a flat buckle collar.

- Introduce and reinforce the commands "sit" and "come" frequently during the day. Have your pup sit for treats, body handling, meals, and on the umbilical leash. Work on the "come" command by using the umbilical leash and the family in a circle as I describe in talking about your first day together. Don't expect to have her master these commands, just introduce and use them as a part of daily life.

- Scope out friends or neighborhood dog owners for vaccinated healthy dogs for your pup to meet.

- Take her to the mall and to a downtown street for socialization, but carry her if you see another dog, to protect her from disease during these episodes.

- Stop by your veterinarian's office at least once for the staff (and your vet, if she's available) to give treats to your puppy.

- Introduce the physical challenges of stairs, curbs, and logs to climb over as I described in confidence building.

11–15 weeks

- Make sure your pup is enrolled in a local puppy kindergarten class by this time.

- Get him to the vet for booster shots. Stop by your vet's at least twice during this time for informal treats and petting.

- Begin a "formal" training session of five minutes or so every evening. Put your pup on a leash and walk her around your backyard several times. Introduce the "down" command, but focus on the "sit" and "come" commands.

- Keep the socialization going with other safe dogs, different people, and locations. Do at least two sessions a week of "confidence-building" exercises over obstacles like stairs and logs.

- Check the fit on his collar. He's growing so fast that it might be time for a new one!

16–20 weeks

- If your pup is a middle- or large-sized breed, he is beginning to get bigger and stronger! Make sure that your pet is fully under your control. This is your last chance to get these basics down before you have a much bigger, much stronger pet on your hands. If there is any question, get a trainer to help you.

- Get your pup's last set of booster shots.

21–32 weeks

- Consider early neutering for dominant male pups.

- Be prepared for serious chewing. Your pup's baby teeth are loosening, and new teeth are beginning to come in. Make a point of giving your pet some new toys to chew on during this time. An ice cube or two a day to gnaw on will soothe his aching gums as well.

- Be sensitive to a second "fear imprint" stage during this period.

- Continue obedience training. Your pup should know the "come," "sit," "down," and "leave it" commands by now.

- Spay your female pup.

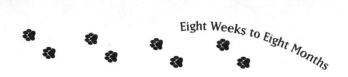

Puppyhood is a wonderful time, to be enjoyed. Take lots of pictures of your puppy in all his funny growing stages. Collect her little teeth as they fall out. Keep his first collar to compare it in size to the much larger one he will someday wear. Even take her paw print and frame it! Save the memories of this special time; your pup will grow up fast enough.

Eleven-month-old Spud is a typical canine teenager: enthusiastic, full of energy, and capable of destroying everything in his path! *Courtesy of Jenny Eddy*

5
Adolescence—Eight to Eighteen Months
Remember, It's Only a Phase

Adolescence is the time when many dog owners seriously reconsider the decision to have a canine in their lives. Picture all the annoying habits of human teenagers taking doggie form.

He's enthusiastic, even hyperactive, and may have surprising physical powers—like being able to leap on top of the kitchen table after food in a single bound! He may be so distracted by the world around him that you start to feel unimportant. He's not even looking his best. The once-compact body may have exploded into an awkward composition of parts. His feet and ears are enormous. His hind end is higher than his front end. His wagging tail has become a device to destroy everything in its wake.

Although your patience and commitment to dog owner-ship may be tried to its utmost during adolescence, there is a payback. If you can continue the leadership, training, and socialization you started with your baby during puppyhood, you will minimize the annoyances of adolescence and be well on your way to creating the canine companion you desire.

Adolescent Problems

During adolescence a dog's inherited personality begins to come out, and the pup tries out adult behaviors for the first time. Frequently, these are not welcome behaviors. Your male pup may try to mount your knee, or growl and bark at strangers territorially. Your female, who was friendly as a pup, may have become shy and skittish as an adolescent.

Whether canine teens start trying annoying behaviors out of raging hormones, hyperactivity, or inherited temperament, you have to live with them and work through the problems. Here is a quick guide to many of the most annoying adoles-cent behaviors, and suggestions for dealing with them.

MOUNTING

Dogs of both sexes mount other dogs as a display of domi-nance. Male dogs usually mount people as a show of mis-

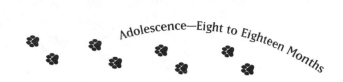

placed sexual hyperactivity. Most pups just try this once, and when you act horrified and prevent them, the behavior goes away. This is not acceptable behavior and should not be permitted under any circumstances.

When your dog reaches for your leg, quickly withdraw it and then distract him with another command like "sit" or redirect his interest into some other activity like playing ball. If he succeeds in grabbing your leg, give him a deafening "NO!" and move away to free yourself. Give him another command like "sit" or "down" and praise him for obeying that command. If he persists, keep him on the leash so that you can give him a stronger correction the next time he tries it.

BARKING

Dogs bark to communicate and when they are bored. Some very vocal dogs bark to relieve anxiety; finding out what is making your dog stressed will help. Bossy dogs bark to demand your attention. Ignoring the "attention barking" will end that behavior. Don't respond at all to your "attention barker"; even yelling at him will reinforce his behavior—some dogs prefer negative attention to no attention at all.

If you leave a dog tied outside or otherwise isolated, he will quickly get bored and may decide to protest his isolation by barking. Not leaving your pet unattended outside for long periods of time will stop this problem.

When an adolescent barks in alarm in your house, teach him the "quiet" command to signal to him that you are in control of the situation. A quick snap of the leash will reinforce your "quiet" command. The second he is still, praise him and redirect his attention to something else with another command like "down."

If your dog barks in the house when you are not at home, you can try a "no bark" collar. These emit a harmless mist of citronella spray when the dog barks, stopping the behavior.

Destructive Chewing

Destructive chewing usually takes place when the owner is away. Behaviorists attribute this to "separation anxiety" and theorize that dogs left at home chew things to calm their nerves. Punishing your adolescent for chewing will only make him more anxious.

Removing all personal items obviously helps, but some dogs then turn to the furniture or baseboards. You can cover the surfaces of these with a deterrent—a product like Bitter Apple, which makes the object taste bad. Some people choose to crate their dogs in their absence. The security of the crate can help, but I have also known dogs who destroyed their teeth trying to chew through the wire mesh of crates. Reestablishing yourself as your dog's leader through obedience training will help the dog feel more secure in this relationship with you, whether you are home

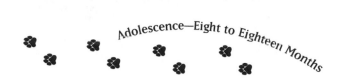

or away. If the problem continues, enlist the help of a trainer or behaviorist.

DIGGING

Most dogs dig for entertainment. It passes the time, and is especially rewarding in the summertime when the cool earth can be flopped in for a snooze. Not leaving your dog out for long, unsupervised periods can prevent digging.

Since digging is normal canine behavior, why not have a section of your yard or garden where you dog is allowed to dig? Call it his "sandbox" if you like. If he really enjoys digging, why deny him? This way you can train him so that he understands it is appropriate to dig only in his sandbox.

PULLING ON THE LEASH

Adolescents love to pull. The world has become very exciting to them, and they want to explore it full speed ahead. Turn to the walking on a leash section in the appendix to review this skill. If your adolescent continues to pull, more serious steps may need to be taken. Under the supervision of a trainer, you may need to use a halter-type head harness, chain-training collar, or pronged collar on your pet. All of these training tools exert physical pressure, and require instruction from a professional and practice to be used correctly.

MARKING IN THE HOUSE

There is a difference between an adolescent male who lifts his leg to mark your sofa and a submissive dog of either sex who leaks urine when stressed or excited. Shy dogs need confidence building, but sassy leg lifters need the opposite. Neutering will help this problem, but establishing yourself as the leader through obedience training and then supervising your pet to prevent the behavior is the real goal.

GARBAGE RAIDING

Since dogs are scavengers, don't be surprised if your adolescent helps himself to an open garbage bag. Securing your waste bin with a lid may solve the problem, but if your canine continues to go into the trash every chance he gets, you might have to set a booby trap for him. Pile light but noisy soda cans precariously on a piece of cardboard up over the trash bin. Support it with another piece of cardboard that can be knocked off. Give him the motive and the opportunity, and get out of the way. The harmless cans should make enough of a clatter to keep him out of the trash in the future.

The Umbilical Leash Grows Up

The single most effective thing you can do to keep an unruly adolescent under control is to have him wear a short leash

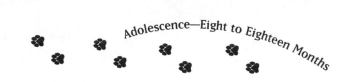

attached to his buckle collar when he is around the house. You don't need to use the full umbilical leash, just keep it dangling so that you can regain control of him. If he jumps up, tries to push through a door, steals something and attempts a getaway, you have an effective way of correcting his behavior. As you growl "no," grab his leash and pull him quickly into a "sit" position to stop whatever disruptive behavior he was doing. Wait a moment, then praise him for the "sit." Keep hold of the leash to maintain control of him as you resume whatever you were doing.

As a puppy, Kimba was always running along behind us, grabbing at our heels. At first we thought he was playing, and we would push him away, but that only made him come back for more. By the time he was an adolescent, it began to get a little scary. He was growing fast and was going to be a big dog. Finally, I started making him wear his leash around the house. When he would reach out with his mouth, I would say, "NO! Sit," pulling up on the leash. This put him in a sitting position and stopped his grabbing. Since I had control of him with the leash, I was able to change his behavior.

—Jason and his adolescent rottweiler, Kimba

Is Your Dog in Heat?

If your female pup is not spayed, she will come into heat during these months. You may notice little red drops appearing on the kitchen linoleum. Female dogs pass through a heat cycle twice a year, beginning around six to ten months of age and continuing through life at roughly six-month intervals. It is critical that you not allow a male dog to breed with your adolescent during this time.

To make things simple, let's call the day you first notice blood, day one. During the first six to sixteen days of what is called proestrus—when the old uterine lining is shed—her discharge will go from pure blood to an almost clear fluid. To protect your rugs, you can buy one of those little doggie sanitary pad ensembles.

When the fluid has changed color, you can be pretty sure that she is in "estrus"—the fertile period of the cycle. Estrus lasts another nine to twelve days, actual ovulation usually taking place within the first forty-eight hours. This is definitely one of those situations in which an ounce of prevention is worth a pound of cure, so keep her inside unless supervised on a leash outside.

When you add the six to sixteen days of proestrus, with the nine to twelve days of estrus, the whole business will take the better part of a month. You can relax when you know a full month has passed. Protect your dog. Don't let a mistake during her heat cycle lead to an unwanted pregnancy.

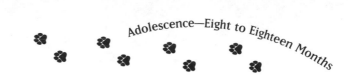

One day a little mutt followed me home from school, and after much talk I persuaded my parents to keep it—at least until the owner turned up or advertised for it. It dwelt among us only one night. Next morning my father took me aside and in a low voice said: "My son, I don't know whether you realized it, but that dog is a female. It'll have to go."

"But why does it have to?" I asked.

"They're a nuisance," he replied embarrassed. "We'd have all the other dogs in the neighborhood around here all the time."

That sounded like an idyllic arrangement to me, but I could tell from my father's voice that the stray dog was doomed. We turned her out and she went off toward a more liberal section of town.

—E. B. WHITE

More Training—More Fun

When you are working with an adolescent, informal play sessions are as important as training sessions. These teenagers "live for play" and you need to divide the time you spend with them between worktime and playtime. In the way that a human teenager's eyes will glaze over during a boring lecture, your canine adolescent will "shut down" if you don't keep your training stimulating. Play with him to keep things inter-

Hide and Seek

If you have a friend or family member to help, games of "Hide and Seek" can exercise your pet and get him using his nose. It is a great game for two or more children to play with a dog, under adult supervision.

You can play this in a fenced-in yard with trees and other things to hide behind, an open field with tall grass, or even inside a house if you don't mind the "mad dash" aspect of it. If you are not in a fenced-in area, make sure your pup keeps her thirty-foot leash on for safety.

Have one person hold the dog while the other one runs and hides either in the tall grass, behind something in the yard, or somewhere in the house. When the person is well hidden, release the dog (holding the end of the thirty-foot leash) and encourage the dog to "find" the person.

Make the first games simple, with the dog actually seeing where the person hides so that she can find him easily. When the dog succeeds, she learns the point of the game. Lots of praise and treats should reward her when she comes up to the hidden person. Gradually make "Hide and Seek" more challenging by blocking the dog's view when the person hides. Always make sure that the dog "succeeds" and gets lots of praise. Repeating this exercise several times will give your dog good exercise while he "works" for you by using his natural abilities. These are the same skills that search-and-rescue dogs use.

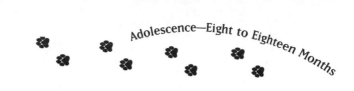
esting, and channel that play enthusiasm into your formal work.

Romping with your teenager before, during, and after your training sessions will do two things: burn off some of the abundant energy her body is producing, and enable her to focus on you during the session. Working on straight obedience for five minutes, then throwing a ball for two minutes, and coming back for five more minutes of obedience will break the monotony and give your work a jolt of fun. Ending a session with something lighthearted—retrieving a ball or stick, an outside game of "Find It!", using a toy or treat, or "Hide and Seek"—will make your pet look forward to your next session together.

Other Energy-Burning Activities

The quickest way to tire your adolescent out is to play games that cause him to run in spurts. Retrieving a tennis ball is probably the best way to do this. I like to bring a tennis racquet and actually hit balls for my dog. Serves, lobs, long shots—they'll all give your adolescent a great workout. Have him bring the ball back to you, but stick an extra ball or two in your pocket in case his retrieve is not as accurate as his chase. Ten to fifteen minutes of this exercise should take the edge off even the most hyper pet.

Strategically positioning yourself at the top of a hill and throwing a stick or ball down the hill for your dog to chase and retrieve is another economical way to burn adolescent energy. The exertion of the uphill run will tire him out twice as fast.

We've got a great hill near our house, and when Kelly gets too nuts, I take her over there and throw a stick downhill so that she has to run back up with it. After five minutes her tongue is lolling, and after ten she is ready to quit. It's the quickest way I've found to tire her out.

—MATT AND KELLY, HIS SPRINGER SPANIEL

Swimming is the perfect exercise for adolescents since it doesn't stress or jar growing bones and muscles. Find a pond,

Working Spud under, over, and around a park bench gives him a great workout while teaching him to focus on me. These exercises are a wonderful introduction to the agility work described in chapter seven. *Courtesy of Jenny Eddy*

A Confidence-Building Course
for Adolescents

Make a course, with jumps, overs, and unders for your adolescent. For example, using the same fallen tree or a park bench:

Ask your adolescent to jump back and forth over the bench three times, then have him do a "sit" to the count of five. After the sit, run him around the bench at a fast "heel" twice clockwise, then reverse and go around twice counterclockwise. Come to a halt next to the part of the bench that can be crawled under and make him lie down to the count of five. Without letting him stand up, encourage him to crawl on his belly under the bench. On the other side, get him up and have him jump onto the bench and balance there for an instant. If he can keep his balance, ask him to walk along the length of the bench, turn around, and walk back if possible. Have him jump off and then sit in front of you to finish. Give him praise and a treat reward.

You can make up little courses like this all the time. They will challenge your pet, encouraging him to focus on you and have fun.

slow river, or beach and give your adolescent a water work-out. Be sure to introduce swimming in a positive manner, as I describe in the next chapter, and follow the water safety advice listed in the appendix.

The confidence-building exercises I described in the last

chapter are especially useful for adolescents. Any activity that uses your pup's physicality and causes him to focus on you is perfect for this age group. By now you should have surmounted the obstacles in the local playground, and worked over, under, and across all the fallen trees. Always have one eye out for interesting new objects. Ideally, you might take this training to the next level—joining a dog club that offers an agility course. Turn to chapter seven for more information on agility work.

Early Displays of Dominance

A protective, territorial response to intruders and guarding food and toys is normal canine behavior. In the wild these instincts are necessary for survival. But in your human home these behaviors can lead to your dog biting a guest or family member.

Wolf cubs and dominant domestic pups can begin to exhibit these behaviors as early as thirteen weeks of age, but the behaviors are more visible during adolescence. Young canines begin to feel protective of themselves or their things. They may object to punishment, bark at strangers, or growl when you try to take a toy away from them.

This often comes as a surprise to owners, or is treated with pleasure since they "wanted a good watchdog." But for your pup to survive in your world, you need to control these protective impulses. After all, you, not your dog, decide who enters your home, who controls the toys, food, and furniture.

I discuss the issues surrounding dog aggression in the following chapter, but it is important to first recognize these behaviors as the beginning of a problem instead of "cute" misbehavior on the part of your teenager. Increase the control you have over your pet through obedience training and socialization—not by brute discipline.

VISITORS AND GUARDING FOOD OR TOYS

Adolescents may need to be specifically trained to greet visitors to your home. Your pup's instincts tell him to alert his pack to the intruder, and protect them from the threat. If you want him to behave differently, you must train him.

Once your pup begins to guard his home, he may also become more assertive with you. The door will become a very important place. Visitors—intruders, to your pup—enter here, and the order in which the pack exits or enters the door ranks the members. This means that if you allow a dominant pup to go through a doorway before you do, you are giving him the signal that he outranks you. In a wolf pack, the leaders are always physically ahead of the followers—that's how they lead. Make sure that you precede your adolescent though doorways.

If your teenager is increasingly aggressive to visitors, practice having a friend come to your door and give treats to your pup. Always focus your attention on the visitor and tell your pup to "sit" for treats from the stranger. Praise your pup for acting friendly to the visitor, and reprimand him with a "No! Quiet!" and a tug on the leash if he keeps barking or growling.

Domino, our dalmatian, started to growl and bark at anyone who came to our door. At first I thought it was normal, but when the barking got fierce, I realized that we had a real problem. I started taking Domino to obedience classes, and the trainer came over one evening to work on his doorway manners.

She had me keep Domino on the leash in the house before she rang the bell, then when she rang and we went to the door, Domino had to sit down. I couldn't open the door until he was sitting still. Every time I started to open it he would stand up and I would have to close the door again and make him sit.

Finally, he stayed sitting, and I opened the door. He started barking at her, and she told me to tell him "No! Quiet," which I did. When he stopped barking, he got a treat. Well, that stopped his barking right away, because he loves treats. Then she gave him a few treats for sitting still and being quiet and his tail began to wag. We practiced putting the whole thing together— the sit before the door opens, staying seated, and no barking—as she went in and out that evening. The next day he was better, but the trainer had to come back again, and I had to get other friends to help Domino practice until he was able to greet people with a wagging tail. I still feel that Domino would protect me if an unfriendly person came to the door, but now I don't worry that he will nip one of my friends.

—SARAH AND DOMINO, HER ONE-YEAR-OLD DALMATIAN

"Guarding" food dishes or toys is another early sign of a dominant dog. Deal with these by regularly *adding* a treat or an extra portion to your adolescent's bowl when he is halfway through a meal. This way, he associates human hands near his food as a positive thing. Accustom teenage canines to surrendering favorite toys to you with an exchange. Offer another toy as a distraction in a kind of "bait and switch" until your dog surrenders things readily.

With these ideas I hope you will have the basics you need to survive your pet's teenage months. No matter what creative things he or she comes up with, try and deal with them in a positive way. Your hard work got her through puppyhood, and it will get her through adolescence as well.

6

Young Adulthood—Eighteen Months to Three Years

Your Pet Evolves

By young adulthood, your dog has matured. If you pay close attention, you may notice him being able to carry ideas over from one thing and apply them to another. This will be especially evident if you are involved in obedience, where you regularly work your dog through a prescribed routine.

Work Out Together

Your young adult is as athletic and full of energy as he will ever be. Dogs derive the same benefits from exercise that we enjoy. How much exercise does your dog need? Studies done

in a lab situation showed that a beagle could dogtrot steadily on a treadmill for seventy-five minutes, bad news for the dog owner who expects a walk around the block to tire out her canine young adult. However, if the beagle was forced to lope—going from the energy-conserving dogtrot to a slightly faster gallop—*he tired within fifteen minutes.*

Fast walking, jogging, swimming, Rollerblading, or biking with your pet is a great solution. Although the running exercises are best suited to the medium- to large-sized, longer-legged breeds, any dog can benefit from aerobic conditioning. Obviously unathletic breeds like English bulldogs should not be pushed to exercise too much. Here are some tips about exercising together safely, but if you have any questions about

Young adult Gus is game for anything, but with his thick coat, care must be taken in hot weather to keep him from overheating during exercise. *Courtesy of the author*

your pet's soundness or limits, consult your veterinarian.

Dogs suffer muscle aches, pains, and other exercise-related injuries just as their owners do. You must condition your pet for strenuous exercise in the same way you would condition yourself, starting off slowly, gradually increasing the intensity of the workout. Don't make your young adult a "weekend warrior" who is dragged around the park a few times every Saturday when you get your bike out. He'll start off enthusiastically, but end up tender-footed, tired, and possibly overheated, never mind stiff and sore for the next few days. Instead, introduce a regular exercise program slowly and carefully.

Moby and I started jogging together, and we both lost some weight. First we walked fast, then we jogged some and walked some, and now we can jog for thirty minutes without stopping. I'm so happy, I'm starting to wonder if they let dogs run along in mini-marathons.

—JOHN AND HIS BLACK LAB, MOBY

While you can go out and buy a new pair of running shoes when your old ones wear out, your dog is stuck with his pads. As tough as they look, a dog's paws may become worn and begin to bleed after as little as ten minutes of running on pavement. Again, start slowly. Foot pads will toughen up quickly if you give your dog three or four days' rest between your initial short runs.

Teaching Your Dog to Swim

Although all dogs have a natural instinct to move their legs to keep themselves afloat, some are naturally good swimmers and others require introduction to the water. Under no circumstances should you throw your pet off a dock or into a pool to teach him to swim; this can permanently traumatize him.

If your dog is reluctant to go near the water, try a little bribery. Serena's mother, Phebe, loved the water, but Sina needed the "Magic Floating Dog Treat Trick" to entice her into the deep. I simply stood by a pond and tossed dog biscuits (which float) into the water. She waded in and gobbled them up. I gradually threw the biscuits farther and farther from the shore until her wading naturally turned into swimming. You can do the same thing with a stick or tennis ball if your dog loves to retrieve. The key is to go step-by-step so that your dog does not panic when he suddenly finds himself in water over his head.

Heat is your dog's other enemy. Don't run him on a hot day—in humid weather, that means eighty-five degrees and over. The thickest paw pads are no match for hot summer pavement! Before you set off on your run, take the time to check the surface temperature of road. If the asphalt is too hot for you to touch, don't risk your dog's paws. Dogs don't sweat as we do, and cannot cool themselves down when they become overheated. If their body temperature goes up even two degrees from their normal temperature of 101–102, they can get heatstroke.

Before you exercise, be sure your pet is wearing a flat buckle collar or, better yet, a chest harness. He should be trained to "heel," meaning that he must run easily at your side, *not* weaving or crossing in front of you. Use a regular leather or nylon six- to eight-foot leash rather than a flexi-leash, which can expand and pull you off balance when your dog suddenly veers after a squirrel.

When roller-skating with your dog, you'll have to be much more aware of safety than you would be by yourself. *Always* be prepared to stop—FAST! Don't get going so speedily downhill that your dog can't keep up. You will probably have to "ride" the brake on the down hills, wearing it out more quickly, but don't get ahead of your dog! Practice braking when your dog is pulling hard. You might consider *adding a brake* to your other skate so that you'll be ready for anything. An accident can happen in an instant. The more practiced and steady you are, the safer you'll both be.

If you plan to bike with your pet, I suggest installing an arm off the body of your bike that attaches to your dog's leash. These are available from **Springer** at 800-BIKE-K9s, and **K9 Cruisers** at 800-K9-CRUISer, and allow you to ride along without the fear of your dog crossing in front of you and causing a crash. Always bike at a comfortable speed for your pet, and check his pads for signs of wear and tear.

While exercising, keep your pet properly hydrated by giving

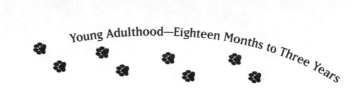
him a chance to drink water every twenty to thirty minutes. You may need to bring water with you in a doggie canteen, or teach your pet to lap from park drinking fountains.

Having your canine join you for a jog or Rollerblading can be a pleasure and a great stress reliever—for both of you.

Confidence or Overconfidence?

I began to talk about aggression in the last chapter, and it may not have been a problem for you during adolescence. Unfortunately, that may not mean that your pup will never exhibit these behaviors. The self-confidence of young adulthood can cause dogs to begin to object to things. Barking or growling is a dog's way of saying, "Don't do that" or "Get out of here." These "verbal cues" are warnings to signal their displeasure. Usually dogs resort to biting only when their other signals are ignored.

Canine aggression takes many forms, but they all boil down to a dog objecting to something and acting aggressively to change the situation. Let's take a look at some of the most common types.

PROTECTIVE BEHAVIOR

I'm at my wits' end. He was the sweetest puppy you ever saw, but ever since he turned two, I noticed him getting really protective. Now he's almost three, and he just nipped a neighbor's kid who was playing with my son. I can't risk leaving him

*alone with them anymore. Maybe if we neuter him he'll calm
down.*

—Sheila, talking about her Lab-doberman mix, Ranger

Sheila is rightfully worried. Ranger has become increasingly
protective of the family and now aggressively defends them
from what he perceives as potential threats. A pet dog of a
protection breed, Ranger should have been neutered at the
appropriate age—six to eight months—and the problem
might have been avoided entirely. Dictated by his genes and
his hormones, an "intact" male of a protection breed is
almost *certain* to mature into a very protective individual.
When making a neutering decision at six months, dog owners
need to consider all the life stages the dog will pass through,
not the sweet pup he is at six months, but the mature dog he
will become. Neutering an adult dog who is already exhibit-
ing dangerous behavior is "too little, too late."

A dog like Ranger, of protection or working bloodlines,
requires much more training and supervision than a "softer"
dog. Training and continuing to work any dog throughout his
life span—not just teaching him to "come" at six months and
then assuming that the job is done—not only keeps him obedient but keeps the "chain of command" clearly defined and
builds a deep bond of respect and communication between
owner and dog. Sheila has probably not worked with Ranger,
or reinforced the idea that she is in charge of him and the family, since he was a young dog. She has allowed the lines of

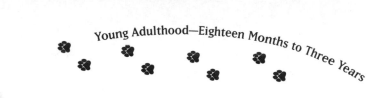
dominance to blur, and Ranger himself has taken control, asserting his authority by biting children he is suspicious of.

At this point, Sheila needs to enlist the aid of a serious trainer who will help her regain control of Ranger and reestablish herself as head of the family. She also needs to monitor Ranger, not placing him in situations where he has the opportunity to act inappropriately on his protective drive.

Territorialism

Guarding property is normal canine behavior. Dogs guard what is theirs, or what they *perceive* to be theirs. The "perceive" part is where things get tricky.

Dogs take property in the broadest, most fluid sense. From their favorite bone to your yard and even the fire hydrant ten blocks away, they may choose to defend their territory. If you allow your pet on the furniture, he might begin to view a favorite chair or your bed as his alone. This urge to guard is a huge component of a dog's psyche.

Imbi Kiiss, a dog trainer on Cape Cod, told me a story of how a dog's territorial urges took over a whole family. Imbi got a call from a family with a young adult Lab mix. As she questioned the owner, the profile emerged of a very dominant dog. Overwhelmed by the Lab's strength and hyperactivity, the family had been unable to control him since he was an adolescent. Choosing to overlook his bossy behavior, the owners had pulled back at every challenge from the pet, making the problem worse. "We really love him," the father assured Imbi.

"Does he have any toys or pieces of furniture that he thinks of as his?" Imbi asked, trying to get a handle on how bad things were.

"Oh, yes, that's why we're calling," responded the father. "He has a special chair he likes. We call it the 'throne.'"

Oh, no, thought Imbi, rolling her eyes.

"At first we couldn't sit in the throne without getting growled at," the father continued. "Then we couldn't sit in chairs near the throne. Now we aren't allowed in the room at all. The problem is that this room connects to the breezeway to our garage, and if he's on his throne, we can't get to the car." Imbi went to help the captive family that afternoon.

Robin Kovary, a trainer in New York City, tells a story of two adults who were dominated by their white poodle. This ten-pound dog growled and snapped at her owners if they thwarted her in anything she wanted to do. Robin was only called in when the dog began jumping up on the dinner table and walking around and eating off their plates.

The good news is that dogs with these problems respond very well to an owner reasserting his leadership. Usually they have taken control of the household because their owner did not offer them the leadership they needed. When Robin snapped a leash on the dinner-plate–raiding ten-pound poodle and handed it to the one-hundred-fifty-pound owner, the balance of power in the relationship changed. Having a professional help you reestablish your leadership with your dog through guidance, boundary setting, and training can turn things around very quickly.

Doggie Push-Ups

A great way to control your dog and refocus his attention is to have him do a few push-ups. Start with your dog on a leash sitting next to you. Give him the "down" command. As soon as he lies down, give him a "sit" command, followed by another down. Treats and praise should follow several "push-ups," but should not interrupt them. Up, down, up, down; by the end of several repetitions, your dog will be panting and focused entirely on you!

Aggression Toward Visitors

Obviously, humans *want* dogs to guard things. One of the reasons we domesticated dogs was to have them do just that, guard our property. We genetically designed all of the "protection" breeds to be suspicious of strangers.

Owners frequently allow their dogs to be aggressive to strangers because they want a good watchdog but don't realize the potential liability of owning an aggressive pet. If you want a watchdog, specifically train your dog to guard by doing "protection work" or *schutzhund* with a trainer, as I describe in chapter seven. This way, you will be in control of your dog's actions. Without training, a dog who is hostile to a burglar may be equally as aggressive to the Girl Scout selling cookies.

If your dog shows any signs of preventing visitors access to your home—from the mailman to the neighborhood children who show up on the back step—regain control of the situation. Do the exercises I describe in the previous chapter and contact a trainer. Protect your pet by keeping him safely away from visitors until the trainer can intervene.

Fear-Induced Aggression

If a dog is afraid or suspicious of something and is not given a chance to retreat, he may react aggressively out of fear. To avoid situations in which your dog may lash out, learn to read his fearful body language. When you see him stiffening or shrinking away from something, take the pressure off. Give him space by physically moving him away. When he has relaxed, try to distract your pet with some positive obedience commands.

Even if your shy or nervous dog has never bitten, respect her emotions. Fearful dogs must be given every chance to gain confidence. Many small commands as simple as "sit" or "come" should be given daily in a nonstressful, nonjudgmental manner. At each opportunity the dog should be encouraged and praised, never criticized. As you do this work, supervise her to prevent her from feeling trapped and lashing out. This process is not just an attempt to protect yourself from the liability of owning a "fear biter," it is a gift to your dog. She will enjoy her life much more if she is not stressed by her environment.

Many anxious or fearful dogs can be helped through massage. Acupressurists report a spot at the top of the dog's head,

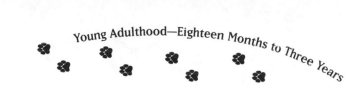

between the ears, that, when pressed, has a calming effect. Find the bump at the crown of the skull and move your finger toward your dog's nose. The pressure spot is the small indentation just in front of it. Putting your dog into a "sit" and stroking his fur, then working up to that pressure point, can calm him down when he is fearful.

Maggie became increasingly shy and skittish as she got older. By the time she was two she would wet if anyone came in the house, and hide behind my legs in public. It looks terrible to see a big dog like a shepherd cringing like that, but what could I do? One time a man tried to do the "Come on, don't be afraid" routine with her. He crouched down and sort of crawled after her as she fled behind me to get away from him. When she had gone as far as the leash would let her, she turned around and snapped. Thank God she missed him, but it was terrible. After that I realized that she could be dangerous, and I took her to a behaviorist. With his help, Maggie has improved, especially in the house, but I had to realize that this is just who she is, it's not a phase. As her owner, I need to keep her stress level down, and protect her from the damage her fears can cause her to do.

—BARBARA AND HER GERMAN SHEPHERD, MAGGIE

Becoming the New Owner of a Young Adult

If you have decided to find your canine companion through a shelter or rescue group, there is a good chance that a young

adult or mature dog has joined your home. There is a common misperception that all shelter pets have been "abused." But people usually surrender their pets because they underestimated the amount of care and time dog ownership requires.

You may worry that by adopting an older dog you are asking for nothing but veterinary bills as the dog ages. But, actually, a dog who is healthy in young adulthood is more likely to stay healthy than a puppy with an unknown medical future. Even a five- or six-year-old dog can offer you five to eight more years of companionship.

Dogs who have had another home before yours go through a period of adjustment and you should reserve judgment on your new dog for at least three months. Address the problems that may arise, but don't give up on your new pet. Most rescue groups and animal shelters offer continuing advice, and some even offer training classes.

Young adulthood is a wonderful time in your dog's life. Keep up the training to stay on top of his changing needs, and make sure he has enough exercise so that you both keep your sanity!

7
Adulthood—Three to Eight Years
Your Complementary Companion

An adult dog has more to give than ever before. Adults are mature, focused, and secure in their relationship with you. Why not explore some of the many activities available to you and your pet at this time? Your bond will only grow deeper as you work together.

Here is an overview of some of the terrific events and competitive activities you can do with your dog. While many owners begin this kind of work early in their dogs' lives, you can begin at any time. All dogs can learn new tricks!

Complementary Companions

If you both enjoyed the obedience part of learning to live together, you might consider further projects that use that training dynamic. Your options include programs like the Canine Good Citizen test; competitive obedience through the various breed registries; tracking and working competitions; pet therapy programs; and recreational activities like Frisbee and lure coursing. All these activities are an expression of the rapport between you and your pet.

Winston, a mastiff, exudes the confidence and presence of adulthood.
Courtesy of the author

CANINE GOOD CITIZENS

The American Kennel Club established the Canine Good Citizen test to promote and encourage responsible dog ownership. Open to mixed breeds as well as purebred dogs, the CGC is a noncompetitive certification program that displays a dog's good manners and sound temperament.

The test comprises ten exercises that evaluate your dog's obedience, responsiveness, and general deportment. These include a knowledge of basic obedience commands as well as several temperament evaluation tests—walking calmly through a crowd, being approached and petted by a stranger, encountering a strange dog, reacting to distractions, and being left alone. All dogs who pass receive an official AKC Canine Good Citizen Certificate (we have Serena's up on the refrigerator!), a personalized CGC ID tag, and a wallet card for you.

Frequently, training groups will offer classes specifically geared toward the CGC test. If you sign up for a basic obedience class and want to try for CGC, inform your instructor and he or she should be able to guide you with exercises that will "groom" you, and your dog, for the test. To get more information, contact the **American Kennel Club,** Attention: Canine Good Citizen Program, 5580 Centerview Drive, Suite 200, Raleigh, NC 27606, 919-233-3600; http://www.akc.org/.

I was so proud of Amber when she got her CGC. She came to us as a mature dog from setter rescue, and she was very nervous. It took her a long time to relax in our home, and the first

*few months were a little tough. I started training her to help
her bond to me, but when she passed her Canine Good
Citizenship test, it made me feel like all the hard work had
been worth it. She's definitely my dog now, and I love her.*

—EMILY, TALKING ABOUT HER IRISH SETTER, AMBER

OBEDIENCE COMPETITIONS

The American Kennel Club, 919-233-3600, the United
Kennel Club, 100 East Kilgore Road, Kalamazoo, MI 49001,
616-343-9020, and the American Mixed Breed Obedience
Registration (AMBOR), 205 1st Street S.W., New Prague,
MN 56071, 612-758-4598 sanction dog shows and matches
where you can compete in obedience on several levels. The
matches are a smaller, less formal version of the shows, where
you can practice under show conditions. The results are not
counted toward any awards or titles. The shows are grander
affairs, and the results count.

There are three successively more challenging obedience
levels, with titles or degrees, which your dog can win. *Novice,*
or Companion Dog (CD), consists of six basic exercises: heel
on the leash, heel free, stand for examination, a long recall, a
long sit, and a long down-stay. *Open,* or Companion Dog
Excellent (CDX), comprises seven exercises: heel free, drop to
a down-stay on a recall, retrieve an object, retrieve over a
high jump and then a broad jump, a long sit, and a long
down. *Utility,* or Utility Dog (UD), the most challenging, is

performed silently, with the dog working from hand signals rather than voice commands, and includes scent discrimination, jumping, retrieving, and a group examination.

To earn an obedience degree, a dog must get three "legs," at three separate dog shows. A "leg" is won if your dog obtains a score of 170 or higher out of a possible 200 points, and more than 50 percent credit on each exercise.

Sounds easy? Not! Blowing any single exercise costs you the class, even though the rest of the performance might have been flawless. It can be as nerve-racking as Olympic ice skating.

But obedience competitors are a dedicated group. I had a girlfriend with a particularly clever Husky named Boris. She had trained this dog to within an inch of his life, so that Boris was performing the routine for the CD title in his sleep. Confident that he would easily win his three legs in three successive shows, she planned on kicking back and relaxing for the rest of the summer.

At the first show, Boris heeled perfectly, but when she commanded him to come to her on the recall, he looked mystified, as though he had never heard the word "come" in his life. Zero credit, one leg blown. They continued, and Boris did the other exercises perfectly. All the next week they practiced recalls. At the next show, he heeled on the leash, came on the recall, but when she took his leash off for the free heeling, Boris wandered out of the ring to make friends with the dogs waiting on deck. She was halfway through the heeling pattern before she realized that he wasn't with her.

Another leg blown. More off-leash heeling practice all week. The third show brought perfect performances in heeling and recall, but when the judge approached him for the stand for examination, Boris threw himself on the ground and rolled over to have his stomach scratched. No credit for the stand, no leg.

This continued through June, then into July and August. Every week she diligently trained Boris, paid the entry fees and schlepped to a show, and every weekend he found some new and unpredictable way to get zero credit on at least one of the exercises. He would execute everything else flawlessly, and never messed up the same way twice. It was impossible to prepare for his "flunk of the day" and thus impossible to train around the problem. The only thing for sure was that he *would* flunk something.

At summer's end, when she and Boris had been to no less than fifteen shows—yes, every weekend, plus the "Three Shows in Three Days" long weekend in Vermont—without a single leg to show for their efforts, Boris finally broke her spirit. It was the last exercise; he had done everything else perfectly. His sits had been straight, his stand for examination as solid as a rock, his recall like an arrow to the mark, his long sit composed and regal. I could see her thinking, "Finally, we'll get one!"

Two minutes into the five-minute long down-stay, Boris's tail began to wag. Technically he was still lying down, but he began to inch imperceptibly toward her, his tail thumping. It

was more like a wiggle than an actual crawl, and you had to look hard, and note landmarks, to see him covering ground, but he was soon a full body length out of the line with the other dogs. When the judge called, "Return to your dog," at the end of the five minutes, Boris had traversed the ring and lay at her feet, smiling up at her. Another zero.

What can you do with a dog like that? His sense of either whimsy or theater overrode his will to perform a routine he had done a million times before. He had probably enjoyed all the attention and travel the summer had brought. Boris just couldn't resist creatively embellishing the prescribed routine. It was the entertainer in him. Impossible, unreasonable, completely Boris. She knelt down and gave him a hug.

If Boris's tale hasn't filled you with dread of the hidden "showman" in your dog, and if you and your dog find working together mutually enjoyable, I urge you to go further with training. Entering obedience competitions and pursuing titles with your dog is very rewarding. The most natural way to become involved is to train with a professional or an obedience club. Clubs are not-for-profit groups and usually have a good trainer on board, as well as members who compete regularly themselves and have had years of practical experience. Obedience clubs usually host seminars on canine topics, give obedience demonstrations in their community, and have social events—there's *always* a doggie costume party at Halloween! Contact the American Kennel Club for a list of obedience clubs in your area.

THERAPY DOGS

What could be more rewarding than sharing the love and happiness your dog provides with someone confined to a nursing home or with a child in a special-education setting? A therapy dog program offers you this chance. Once you are certified and registered with one of the therapy dog organizations, you and your dog will be able to regularly visit hospitals, nursing homes, and special-education programs at schools, spreading good cheer or just supplying someone with an understanding gaze and a furry neck to hug.

Certifying your dog for therapy work includes taking the Canine Good Citizen test, but with elements that reflect what your dog might encounter in a nursing home or hospital. There is generally a wheelchair your dog must approach and stay near without fear, a food distraction—to teach even the most "food-oriented" pet to ignore a patient's lunch tray—and other potential disturbances such as noisy children, canes, and walkers. Obviously, you should acclimate your dog to some of these potential distractions before the test, and you can even prepare, as you would for the Canine Good Citizen test, with a private trainer or group.

You can receive more information about therapy dog work from the governing bodies: **The Delta Society,** 321 Burnett Avenue South, 3rd Floor, Renton, WA 98055, 206-226-7357; **Therapy Dogs International,** 6 Hilltop Road, Mendham, NJ 07945, 201-543-0888, E-mail: TDI@GTI.net, or http://www.

TDI-DOG.org; and **Therapy Dogs Incorporated,** P.O. Box 2786, Cheyenne, WY 82003, 307-638-3223.

TRACKING AND TRIALING

In addition to obedience competitions, the American Kennel Club sanctions tracking tests resulting in Tracking Dog (TD) or Tracking Dog Excellent (TDX) titles. Any breed may compete in tracking, following a scent over a prescribed course, and it's a wonderful way to use the amazing scenting ability of your dog.

People don't realize how much dogs love scent work. Penny and I started doing scent discrimination for our Utility Dog title, but when I saw how much she enjoyed using her nose, we just kept on training. Now she is on the way to getting her TDX.

—MARGE AND HER SHELTIE, PENNY

Field trials test the ability of the sporting breeds to continue to perform their original function. Hundreds of field trials are held all over the country each year. If you have purchased a puppy from a breeder who competes in trials, he or she will guide you. Should you decide to pursue your dog's inbred talents without a breeder's guidance, information is also available through the AKC and the various breed clubs that sponsor competitions appropriate for their breed.

LURE COURSING

For all of you out there with retired racing greyhounds, Afghans, basenjis, borzois, or any of the other "sight hounds," *this is for you!* Lure coursing allows your dog to vent all that pent-up running/hunting drive he rarely gets to vent within the confines of your lifestyle. The dogs chase a strip of plastic, meant to represent prey, attached to nylon cord stretched in a series of turns and straightaway over a prescribed course, from 500 yards to over a mile long. Aside from taking your hound to the desert and setting him on some hapless jackrabbit, this may be the only time you see him at a full gallop, racing the wind and pursuing game, as his ancestors did for centuries. You can get more information about lure coursing from the **American Sight Hound Field Association,** 2234 Walnut Avenue, McKinnleyville, CA 95521.

CHANNELING ALL THAT CANINE ENERGY: AGILITY WORK

As we all know, dogs just love to jump over, crawl under, and clamber around on things. Agility courses, which are a combination of a doggie playground and an obstacle course, make the most of these "talents." Working through the various jumps, tunnels, seesaws, and ramps builds your dog's trust and confidence in you, strengthening the bond you share. In competition, you race the clock to get through the

course quickly and cleanly, but just working your dog through the obstacles without competing is fun for both of you. The **United States Dog Agility Association,** P.O. Box 850955, Richardson, TX 75085, 214-231-9700, will send you a list of agility clubs or events in your area.

IS YOUR DOG A FRISBEE DOG?

Yes, what you thought of as a convenient way to exercise your dog has become a sport! The Friskies company has taken the sport on, sponsoring the annual Friskies Canine Frisbee Championship. The most famous canine Frisbee athlete was the purebred whippet Ashley, owned and trained by Alex Stein (it is legend that Stein fed Ashley, from puppyhood, out of an upside-down Frisbee!). Stein has put out a manual for training your dog to be a Frisbee champ, along with information about competitions; call **Friskies,** 800-423-3268, or write to: **Friskies Competitions,** 4060-D Peachtree Road, Ste. 326, Atlanta, GA 30319.

SCHUTZHUND

The sport of *Schutzhund* (German for "protection dog") is made up of three elements—tracking, obedience, and protection—and there are three levels of difficulty: Schutzhund I, Schutzhund II, and Schutzhund III.

Originally designed to test the courage and intelligence of

German shepherd dogs, Schutzhund work is performed today by many different breeds. Any type of dog can be trained to do Schutzhund, but it is serious business and should not be entered into casually. Training for the protection component includes accessing and channeling your dog's aggressive side, since he must be able to defend you on command. This door to your dog's aggression is *not* one that you want to open unless you are *fully* prepared to take responsibility for the consequences.

If you are interested in pursuing the discipline, the best way is to find a local Schutzhund club and begin attending their meetings and training sessions. You can find out more about the sport by contacting **United Schutzhund Clubs of America, 3704 Lemay Ferry Road, St. Louis, MO 63125**, the governing body in this country.

As you can see, there's a lot more to do with your dog than just walking around the block! Channel his energy through an activity and get the competitive juices flowing for *both* of you!

Adding a Second Dog to Your Life

Adulthood is the best time in your pet's life to acquire a second dog. If you wait until your dog is older and becoming feeble, he may have trouble defending himself from the enthusiasm of a new pup, or keeping his food or toys to himself.

Puppy or older dog? That's up to you. Your current dog

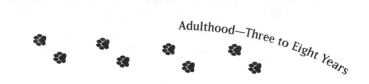

will take him in hand and shape him up either way. However, the transition will go more smoothly if your second dog is the opposite sex of your first. Remember that in a wolf pack dominance is ranked within sexes—so members of opposite genders are less likely to compete for dominance.

First introductions between your dog and the new pet should take place on neutral territory, not on your property. This will minimize your dog's territorial instincts. Have them meet in a park, or even a parking lot, then go home together. Keep the leashes on for the first hour, so that you can control the situation. There will be much sniffing, hackle raising, and possibly growling as your pets feel each other out. Growl right back with a "NO, quiet!" command. Even though you are adding a new member to your pack, you are still the pack leader.

I thought Otis would never forgive me for bringing another dog home. He had been an only dog all his life, and was very bonded to me, but I saw Alice at a shelter and couldn't say no. I had Otie with me in the car, and before the adoption papers were finished, I brought him into the building to meet his new sister just to be sure they would get along. He was fine with her, and I thought things wouldn't be so bad. But when Otis saw that she was coming with us, and getting into "his" car, the hackles went up and he showed her his teeth. As excited as Alice was to jump in the car, she rolled right on her back in submission to Otis. He walked all around her, stiff-legged, as if to say, "If you're coming with us, you've got to do as I say, or else." Then he let her get up and jump in the car. He growled at her, but she just licked at his mouth.

Well, we had to go through that same routine with everything: before Alice could jump out of the car, before Alice could walk in the house, if she wanted to go in the bedroom, before dinner. I ran interference as well as I could, correcting Otis for his behavior, but any time Alice made a move to do anything, he was right on top of her, bossing her around. I finally gave up and decided to let them work it out. I was afraid that she would get fed up and that I would have a dogfight on my hands, but Alice submitted to him each time.

Pally and Tristan share a stick. One of the perks of adding a second dog is getting to watch the wonderful ways the two pets interact. *Courtesy of the author*

It took two weeks for Otis to relax, and now they are best buddies. He still bosses her around, but now I'm beginning to think that Alice likes all the attention Otie gives her.

—BETSEY AND HER TWO MIXED-BREED DOGS, OTIS AND ALICE

Adulthood is a time to enjoy your dog. Take time to be together as complementary companions, going places, working, and exploring the bond that you share.

8
Nine Years and Above
Older Dogs, Best Friends

A healthy older dog, like the Frank Sinatra song says, stays "young at heart." As we know from studies on human aging, those who remain physically and mentally active stay that way longer than sedentary folks. The same is true of dogs.

Life with your pet may have settled into a comfortable routine. He brings you your slippers, you pat him absentmindedly. He sits by his dish, you feed him. You may notice a few gray hairs starting to show on his muzzle, but otherwise he is his regular self. Things are going fine, but your life with your dog has settled into a bit of a rut. How do you keep the spark in this relationship?

The Power of Play

Throughout this book I've been talking about how important it is to engage your canine in play. At every age, play breaks down so many barriers and builds so many bonds.

Does your dog need to play? You bet. Researchers spent a summer studying the habits of feral dogs in St. Louis, Missouri. The "pack" consisted of two males and a female who survived on the scraps of food they found in garbage cans. An abandoned building served as their den. They slept during the heat of the day, then foraged through garbage cans all night and into the morning. Dawn always found the pack at a city park, eating the discarded food around the picnic tables.

After the last picnic table in the park was checked, the pack went to a nearby pond for a swim, then took a nap under a tree.

The behavior that followed their nap confounded the researchers.

The dogs spent a joyous hour stalking and chasing squirrels in the park before retiring to their den to sleep for the rest of the day. In two months of observation, they made no kills. The researchers noted that compared to scavenging garbage, hunting squirrels required a significant outlay of daily energy reserves. It was not positively reinforced, since no squirrels were captured or consumed. Why would the dogs continue this futile and exhausting activity?

All creatures, even feral dogs, need fun in their lives. As

grueling as their daily existence was, the swim, nap, and hour of fun chasing squirrels was a bright spot in their otherwise grim reality.

Dogs need play. Even your older pet, who may seem steady and quiet, needs the interaction and release of play or some kind of work that makes him feel useful. So teach your older pet to play "Find It!" as I describe in chapter four, or toss a stick for him, but get him playing again.

Chase, ten years old and going strong. *Courtesy of the author*

New Careers for Older Dogs

This is a great time to introduce your pet to therapy work, as I describe in chapter seven. Imagine how much more powerful it will be for convalescent home residents to have a canine senior bringing them good cheer!

Last year, my mother entered a nursing home, and whenever I went to visit, she would ask how Elsa was doing. So one day I took Elsa with me to the home. She was such a hit that I decided to try and get her therapy dog certification, even though she was ten years old. We found a trainer who made accommodations for Elsa's age, and she passed the first time she took the test! Now Elsa accompanies me every time I go to the home, and I've arranged for two other members of our therapy dog class to join us. Who would have expected Elsa to get a second career this late in her life?

—ROBERTA AND HER GOLDEN RETRIEVER, ELSA

What about teaching your old dog to track? While his hearing may not be the best, and his vision has been better, dogs rarely lose their sense of smell. Tracking is mentally stimulating but does not have to be physically challenging. If a dog can walk and sniff, he can track.

How about adding a daily walk together? If you have a backyard you may never take your dog for walks. He may not have had a leash on since he finished puppy class! Dust the

leash off and go for it. Turn to the appendix if you need a review session. After you work the kinks out, the two of you can share a special time each day promenading together.

The minute I got his old leash out, Scotty's tail began to wag. He stood perfectly still for me to put it on, then grabbed the leash in his mouth with excitement, the way he used to do when he was a pup. He had so much fun that I felt bad for not doing more with him all these years. Now we go for a walk every day.

—TOM AND HIS TWELVE-YEAR-OLD COLLIE MIX, SCOTTY

Making Special Time for Your Older Pet

Be sure that your older pet has the opportunity for time alone with you. Make an "oldsters only" rule, meaning that your younger pets are excluded. Give your aging dog the recognition and dignity of center stage every so often. He will shine with the attention and be less stressed since he won't have to jostle for position.

Why not make a point of giving your old friend special time alone in the house when he can nap undisturbed? Put the youngsters outside, and give him some peace.

A daily massage gives your old pet special attention, while his tension and soreness is relieved. Stroke him the way I describe in chapter 4, going carefully to ensure that your old pet is not flinching beneath your touch.

While human shoulder blades lie flat, a dog's shoulders curve down, connecting his spine to his front legs. Work that area as you would want your own back rubbed. Pay extra attention to the connection of his shoulders and neck. If his hind legs have weakened, this area may have assumed more of the burden of supporting his frame. End with a head rub and a hug.

If your older dog competed in the breed ring or in obedience trials, or participated in other events in her youth, don't leave her at home when you go to matches or shows. Bring her along! Many meets have a "veterans'" class she can enter. If there is no special accommodation for older pets, why not ask the steward at a trial or meet to let your old dog run through the exercises as a "noncompetitor" during a lunch break or at the end of the day? Let her feel as special as she ever did by giving her a chance to show her stuff!

A Stress-Free Zone

One of the things you can do to help extend an old friend's days is to make her life a "stress-free zone." Little stresses, things that cause physical or emotional strain, can cause problems during old age. Your pet simply may not have the resources to combat these strains, so why not try to eliminate them as much as possible?

If your pet has been housed outside, this is the time to bring him inside at night. There is no reason to deny him the warmth and companionship of your home at this age.

To ensure her comfort, make sure your senior has access to a very warm, very soft bed (not necessarily your own!) for resting those old bones.

What about getting a close-coated dog a sweater or a coat to wear outside? As a dog ages, its skin thins, making it more vulnerable to chills. Adding a layer of warmth can't hurt.

If his old fur tends to mat, consider having him shaved for the summer. A soft undercoat will make it easier to find ticks and fleas and will make your daily grooming sessions pleasanter.

These kinds of small accommodations can make your pet's senior years more pleasurable for him.

Acting Out

Dogs have an advantage over us in that they are unaware of their own mortality. A dog does not think, "Only so many years left," the way we do. But they definitely *do* notice their flagging strength or their loss of social stature among other canines. A housebroken dog may be humiliated by "social lapses" like the urine leakage that sometimes accompanies old age.

These changes can cause them to "act out" or regress. A dog who feels he is slipping in your household canine hierarchy may try to reestablish himself by coming down too hard on the younger pets. He may even pick a fight. Keep close tabs on these situations. If you sense friction, limit the time older and younger pets are together and don't leave them unsupervised. No matter who the dominant dog is, *you* will have to soak the punctured leg or pay the bill to stitch up the torn ear.

An older dog may go through a sort of "second puppyhood" as well. He may misbehave to get your attention. You may not believe your eyes when you look outside and see your perfectly behaved older pet digging a giant hole, or catch him chewing a rug. Give him a mild reprimand for his bad behavior, but take these incidents as a sign that your older dog wants your attention. Adding some special time together—through walks, playtime, or training—can give your pet the attention he craves and prevent him from misbehaving to get it.

The Body Ages

As a body ages, cells break down and do not regenerate as effectively as they did in the past. This process brings new health complications. Your older pet may require more frequent veterinary visits to keep him in top form.

Some of the age-related changes you might expect are:

Stiffness or Lameness

Any number of problems can affect an older dog's mobility, from arthritis and bone disorders to spinal cord, disk, and muscle problems. You might find canine acupuncture tremendously effective in reducing your pet's pain and stiffness.

Vision Problems

You may notice that your older pet's eyes look a little cloudy. Is he going blind? Probably not. All old dogs suffer

Following a cataract operation to save her vision, Louise, a seventeen-year-old Corgi mix, was fitted with glasses! Ophthamologist Dr. Susan Kirschner at New York City's Animal Medical Center prescribed corrective lenses for Louise based on the average refraction of a dog's lens. Louise is so comfortable in her glasses that she often falls asleep with them on. *Courtesy of the Animal Medical Center*

132

from nuclear sclerosis—an age-related change that causes the eye's lens to become cloudy but does not interfere with vision to any great extent. Older dogs do lose vision from cataracts in the same way that people do, and they can receive corrective surgery from a canine ophthalmologist. Glaucoma can also be a problem, as can tumors on the eyelid and decreased tear production.

Hearing Impairment

Hearing problems are common in older pets. Whether deafness is caused by chronic ear infections or by sudden, age-related onset, a dog's hearing usually deteriorates slowly. If your dog becomes unresponsive to your commands, you should have it checked out. Don't assume that he is being stubborn or ignoring you on purpose. If he has lost hearing, he is in danger from traffic or other threats.

Lumps and Bumps

Old dogs are very prone to various lumps and bumps in or underneath their skin. Many kinds of cysts, warts, or tumors can be harmless, but each should be checked out by your veterinarian.

Loss of Balance

Aside from weakness, old dogs can lose their balance. This is often caused by an age-related malfunction called old dog vestibular syndrome. The vestibular mechanism controls balance by coordinating the inner ear and the brain. A veterinarian will be able to diagnose this condition or can discern what else might be causing the "dizziness."

Senility

Brain cells age as the body does, and dogs may become forgetful as they get older. Before you blame senility, check for other culprits. Frequently, similar symptoms can be caused by other health conditions like hearing impairment, loss of vision, or physical weakness. For instance, has the dog begun to soil the house because he has "forgotten" his housebreaking? Or has an incontinence problem developed, which a veterinarian could correct with medication? Does he not recognize people quickly because he has forgotten who they are? Or is his vision dimming so that he has begun to rely on how the people smell and sound to identify them? Investigate the possible causes of your dog's behavior before you blame him for "misbehaving."

Solvable Problems

So many advances have been made in canine medicine and husbandry that life spans are actually increasing. However, problems do come up that can seem insurmountable to a dog owner. Tragically, many older dogs are euthanized by their owners when the dogs lose their vision or hearing or become incontinent. The owners see these problems as signs that "it is time," but that is not necessarily the case. Allowances may need to be made, but old dogs can often continue to live for several years. Let's look at these problems.

Blindness

Dogs adjust beautifully to reduced vision. When a dog loses his sight, his other senses work together to replace the eyes as directional indicators. Your pet will probably move slowly and uncertainly at first, but will soon get accustomed to the new condition. He may stumble or knock against things during this process. Acting as though his new condition is normal will give your pet confidence and will help him make the transition to a life without sight.

There are several specific things you can do to help your dog readjust to life with diminished vision. Help him make a "scent picture" in his mind of your house by marking specific objects with different colognes. Mark hard, upright objects like table and chair legs, doorway walls, and closed doors with one specific scent—and be sure to spray it at your pet's nose level. Spray another scent on the floor right before steps or stoops; this cues your pet to step up or down.

Every member of your family should choose to wear some object or piece of jewelry that makes a sound. You will be amazed by how quickly your pet learns to identify family members by sound, and how easily he follows you about.

Loss of Hearing

Deaf dogs can be taught hand signals rather than spoken commands. With the use of treats (he may not be able to hear, but he can smell treats) and a leash or a long line, you can accustom your pet to paying strict visual attention to you. Do this the way I describe teaching the "Watch me!" exercise in the appendix. Instead of the verbal cue "Watch me!," stamp your foot so that your pet feels the vibration, or use a flashlight to get his attention. Using a treat, bring his eyes up to meet your own. Eventually he will turn to you whenever you stamp or shine the flashlight.

Deaf dogs present some serious safety concerns. They can easily wander or can run into traffic. Also, they can be startled and react aggressively out of fear. Always supervise your deaf dog, and cue him as often as possible with floor vibrations or a light.

I thought she just got lazy. Half the time, when I called her, she wouldn't come. Since Molly is only seven, I didn't think of her as old, that's only forty-nine in human years, right? But my vet reminded me that seven is pretty old for an Irish wolfhound. We've been working with a flashlight, and are keeping her on a long leash. I want to keep my girl with me as long as possible.

—MARK, DESCRIBING HIS IRISH WOLFHOUND, MOLLY

Incontinence

As your pet ages, any number of medical complications can cause him or her to lose control of urine or bowel movements. This can be as mild as a little "leakage" when the pet gets up from a nap, to real loss of control. If your old friend becomes incontinent, the best thing you can do is to cheerfully clean up the mess and take your pet to her veterinarian for a checkup as soon as possible. Frequently, this problem can be quickly and successfully treated. My friend Martine's fourteen-year-old dog, Tito, had a leakage problem caused by reduced estrogen levels in her body. She takes a daily hormone replacement that solved the problem immediately.

Special accommodations may need to be made, like installing a doggie door so that the pet can let himself outside to evacuate. Try to find solutions to this problem, as troublesome as it may be.

Paralysis or Weak Limbs

A stroke or accident may leave your dog without the use of his hind legs. Many owners give their paralyzed pets a second chance with orthopedically designed "wheels." A harness secures your pet's front or rear end to a balanced set of wheels, giving him mobility. You can get more information from **K-9 Carts**, P.O. Box 160639, Big Sky, MT 59716, 406-995-3111.

Dogs who become too weak to jump into the car or climb stairs can get help with specially designed ramps. **Petramp, Inc.,** 4727 Lawrenceville Highway, Tucker, GA 30084, 770-934-1053, and **Pet Care with Love, Inc.,** P.O. Box 764, Dept. DF, Glenview, GA 60025, 800-441-1765, both manufacture portable pet ramps.

Despite your older pet's medical problems, why not find a way to keep him loving you a little longer? Does he still know just when to rest his head in your lap and give you a sympathetic lick? Does he still make you smile? Then he is still your best canine friend, the puppy or older pet who joined your life so many years ago, and has shared your joys and sorrows. Enjoy these older years together.

9

Dealing with Your Dog's Passing

There is sorrow enough in the natural way
From men and women to fill our day;
But when we are certain of sorrow in store,
Why do we always arrange for more?
Brothers and sisters, I bid you beware
Of giving your heart to a dog to tear.

—Rudyard Kipling

At one time or another, we will all be faced with the death of our beloved dogs. The specific circumstances and our reactions to the event will vary, but our sense of loss, our grief, will be the same. Had we anticipated this sadness at the outset, we might never have let the squirmy bundle of puppy, or the lonely older dog, share our life. But we did, and now here we are.

Is there a way to make the process of losing your dog less painful? Yes and no. You can't numb yourself to the grief, but you can prepare for it by apprising yourself of the options and

arrangements you may want to make, and seeking help during your own grieving process.

Depending on the circumstances, your pet could be taken from you abruptly, having been hit by a car or having succumbed to a sudden malady like bloat, or you may be asked to nurse him through many months of a prolonged illness. Ultimately, your veterinarian may ask you to make the final decision. It is your responsibility to seek out the emotional support and help that you may need to get through this difficult time.

Options

Many owners choose to walk away, focusing on happy memories of their dog, allowing the vet to take care of the body. But as the tombs of the ancient Egyptians and the Vikings tell us, for thousands of years people have honored the deaths of their pets in a ritual fashion.

Cremation

If you choose to have your pet cremated, the ashes can either be placed in an urn or buried in a small plot at a cemetery. You can also scatter them over a particularly beautiful or meaningful spot. Your veterinarian will be able to arrange the cremation and help you with your plans.

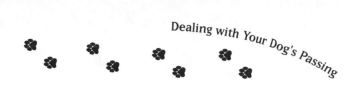

Cemeteries and Memorial Parks

There are beautiful cemeteries and memorial parks all over the nation. Each will collect your pet's remains at either the veterinarian's or your home and will make arrangements for burial. Most will accommodate any type of service you wish to hold for your pet.

Services for your pet can be as simple as a few quiet moments alone in the viewing room before burial to bringing friends, family, and even clergy to a memorial or funeral service. The staff has seen it *all*, so don't feel for a moment that your wishes are "silly." It is fitting, if you so choose, to hold a service where you and your closest friends remember the joy your pet brought to you. You can read a poem, play a piece of music that is meaningful to you, or ask the leader of your church or synagogue to say a few words. I can't guarantee that they will comply, but it doesn't hurt to ask. The cemetery frequently is able to refer you to a spiritual leader who can assist you.

Information about holding a funeral for your pet can be obtained by sending a self-addressed, stamped envelope to **The National Association of Pet Funeral Directors**, 210 Anderson Town Road, Mechanicsburg, PA 19055, or by calling 800-422-1745.

Following a viewing or a service, memorial parks usually encourage owners to accompany the casket or urn to the spot of burial, even to take part in the interment. Of course this is optional, but it can be helpful for you to actually *see* the interment.

You will be able to visit your pet in these beautiful places whenever you wish, and you may find solace in talking to the other pet owners you meet on your visits. Hartsdale Canine Cemetery in New York reports an average of more than five hundred visitors every week, with Christmas and Memorial Day being especially popular. The important thing is to do what feels right to you.

You can get more information and a listing of pet cemeteries in your area from **The International Association of Pet Cemeteries**, 5055 Route 11, Ellenburg Depot, NY 12935.

Memorial Donations

Even after your pet is gone, why not let his memory help other animals by making a contribution in honor of your dog to your local animal shelter, rescue group, or animal hospital?

What About the Pets Left Behind?

If you live in a multiple-animal household, the death of your dog will also affect the other pets. Whether the other pet is another dog, a cat, or a bird, the loss of one member will throw off the balance. You must anticipate and accommodate the grieving of these other creatures. Animals mourn.

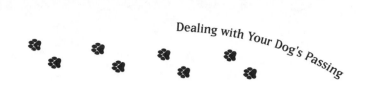

Elizabeth Marshall Thomas, author of *The Hidden Life of Dogs,* spoke at an event I attended, and a woman asked her if dogs feel grief. "Of course they do," she said simply. "Grief and a sense of loss is the price paid by creatures who have the capacity to bond."

Try to spend extra time with the surviving pets. They may be particularly needy, feeling anxiety as well as grief. If they haven't had a chance to see the body and sense the presence of death, all they know is that if one of their pack has disappeared, what might happen to them? Be aware of these issues, and consult a behaviorist if they develop destructive or self-mutilative behaviors. You can expect them to be gloomy and depressed, but keep a close eye on the situation.

If you're considering getting another dog, it's important to work through any feelings you might have that you are betraying your old pet. You must fully understand that a new pet brings a new relationship. Don't get a new dog if you secretly want him to be your old dog all over again. You are putting unfair expectations on him and limiting your own scope of enjoyment. The new pet is likely to bring new and different pleasures, and problems, to your life.

What About You and Your Family's Emotions?

Losing a pet can be every bit as upsetting and depressing as losing any other beloved family member. Whether you live alone with your dog, or have the added challenge of having to explain the loss to a child, it is a particularly difficult process.

Fortunately, wonderful help is available from pet loss grief therapists who specialize in helping clients work through their emotions during and after the loss of a pet.

Several universities sponsor pet loss support help lines staffed by counselors trained in grief therapy. The counselors are frequently either veterinarians or vet students, so they understand the medical issue you may need to discuss. All the hot lines accept messages twenty-four hours a day and return your call the same evening. They will send you written materials and book references on request, as well. Some help lines you can call are:

Pet Loss Support Helpline, 708-603-3994. Sponsored by the Chicago Veterinary Medical Association in conjunction with the Delta Society.

Pet Loss Support Hotline, 916-752-4200. Center for Animals in Society, University of California at Davis.

Pet Loss Support Hotline, 517-336-2696. University of Michigan College of Veterinary Medicine.

Charlene Douglas of Washington State University's People-Pet Partnership Program reports that nearly 80 percent of the people who contact her are grappling with a euthanasia decision. Grieving pet owners also have to face unsympathetic

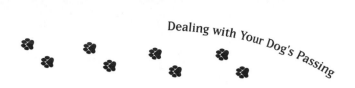

people. "As a society, we're unprepared to talk about death. As a result, people sometimes say silly or dismissive things to cover their own discomfort," Charlene says. "When your grandmother dies, everyone knows the appropriate response is 'I'm sorry, you must feel awful,' but when your pet dies, people are just as likely to say 'Pull yourself together, it's only a dog.'"

Helpful Books

There are many great books on the market about pet loss and grief. Three of them are: *Coping with Sorrow,* by Moira Anderson, M.Ed., Peregrine Press, 1994; *Pet Loss,* by Herbert A. Nieburg, Ph.D., and Arlene Fischer, Harper-Perennial, 1996; and *The Loss of a Pet,* by Wallace Sife, Howell Book House, 1993.

She continues, "Often, pet owners have a stronger grief response from the loss of a companion animal than they do when a human dies. We all deal with emotions differently, and sometimes we can express things over the death of a pet that we bottle up when a human is involved. Don't forget all the secondary losses that occur when your pet dies: the walks, the feeding times, the playtimes. When this animal passes, so do these activities, and there is a lot of time to fill.

"Pet owners in grief need to hear that they're not crazy,"

Charlene says. "Seek out people who are sympathetic to your grief and talk to them. Tell them the story, and then tell them the story again. Know that you are not alone, others do

Courtesy of Jenny Eddy

understand, others do care. The emotions you feel are very natural and should not be denied."

Charlene Douglas can be reached at People-Pet Partnership, College of Veterinary Medicine, WSU, Pullman, WA 99164, 509-335-4569; E-mail, DouglasC@wsu.edu.

Our companion animals give us wonderful gifts: unconditional love, a nonjudgmental attitude, and an ever silent trust. Always remember the gift that your pet gave you, and be thankful for it even when your pet is physically no longer with you.

10
Medical Concerns for the Dog Owner

During puppyhood your pet will visit the veterinarian frequently for her initial inoculations. After that time, most dog owners bring their dogs to the vet just once a year for a checkup. At these visits the veterinarian will examine the dog from the tip of her tail to her ears, administer necessary inoculations, and check the dog's stool for parasites. Any abnormalities may be followed up with other diagnostic tools such as blood tests.

These yearly checkups are an important benchmark of your dog's health and should be kept up. But despite these visits,

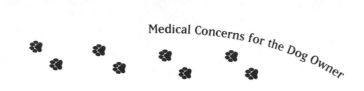

most of the work of keeping your pet healthy falls on your shoulders. You know your dog better than anyone else and will be the first one to notice anything "amiss."

Canine Weight Control

Studies show that between 25 and 40 percent of pet dogs in the United States are obese. Canines in the wild never suffer from this problem. Like human weight problems, canine obesity is linked to other serious health problems. It exacerbates canine hypertension (high blood pressure for dogs), joint and bone disorders like hip dysplasia, spinal problems, and cardiac and reproductive disorders.

Since there are no insurance charts for dogs listing ideal weights, owners and vets rely on a "look and feel" technique to determine a pet's appropriate weight. In all breeds, a dog is considered to be at optimum weight if the ribs can be felt easily (not seen) when you sweep your hand along his flank. Whether he is a pug or a briard, when you look down on your dog's back you should see a slight "hourglass" shape, with a broad chest, shoulders, and ribs tapering to a "waist" before the widening of the hips. If your dog looks like a sausage— straight on either side from the shoulder to the hip instead of curving in to a waist—he needs to lose a few pounds.

Pay attention to your dog's weight. If your vet gives you a stern talk about it, take him seriously and take action. You can help your pet lose extra pounds in several ways:

- Cut down his total daily intake of food by 20 to 30 percent (you bet that includes snacks; don't tell me that the "human food" off your plate does not contain canine calories).

- Change his diet to a low-calorie or "lite" formula for overweight or less active dogs.

- Increase his activity level with fifteen to twenty-five minutes of brisk walking or slow jogging, depending on his capabilities.

- For treats, get rid of the enormous dog bones that you give him. Switch to tiny puppy biscuits—broken in half—or low-calorie slices of apple or hot dog.

Don't put your pet on a starvation diet—he will be as miserable as you would be. Just take it easy on him, gently increase his exercise, and cut down his daily calorie intake until he reaches his ideal weight. Serena's best weight is around eighty-five pounds, but she has weighed as much as ninety-three pounds. I trimmed her down by using the guidelines listed above.

Parasites—Internal and External

Internal parasites like worms usually live in your dog's gastro-intestinal tract, liver, or lungs. They can rob your pet of the nutrition his body needs, cause anemia by destroying his red blood cells, and secrete toxins into his system. Internal para-

(Don't!) Give That Dog a Bone

Dogs love to gnaw on bones. Few things please them so much as sneaking off to a favorite corner with a lovely section of cow femur full of marrow to work on. However, the only really safe bones to give to dogs are well-boiled beef knuckles or a part of the long leg bone. NEVER give your dog any kind of poultry, lamb, pork, or veal bones. These break into brittle shards and can cause serious damage to your pet's mouth and digestive tract. For your dog's safety, you must be vigilant. Even the best-behaved dog is liable to plunder the garbage when sorely tempted, so protect her from herself! Offer safe rawhide (see the sidebar on rawhide later in this chapter) or nylon pseudo-bones as a substitute. Your dog will still try to convince you that it would really be okay to slip him that chicken leg, but don't believe it!

sites can so deplete a dog's system that normal growth and development is stunted. Heartworms, which live in your dog's cardiac system, can be fatal.

The most common types of gastrointestinal parasites are roundworms, tapeworms, whipworms, and hookworms. All can be diagnosed by fecal examination, and can be treated by your veterinarian.

Many dogs are born with worms. Roundworms can be passed from a infected mother dog to her puppies across the placenta during gestation and through her milk. For this reason it is very important that your veterinarian worm your pup repeatedly during his first six months of life. Dogs also get worms by inhaling or swallowing infective worm larvae. Infective-stage larvae is present in the feces of a wormy dog. Keeping your pet from smelling the feces of other dogs is an important way to prevent worms. Regular screening and treatment is the best defense.

Heartworm is carried by mosquitoes. It is a potentially fatal parasite because the adult worms take up residence in the pulmonary arteries and the right side of the heart. If not detected and treated, this leads to hypertension and pulmonary emboli (sudden blockages of blood vessels). Get those heartworm checks every year, and get your dog on preventive heartworm medication. You do not want to have to fight heartworms.

Fleas

The flea bites its host to feed on blood, but spends most of its life span off the host, in the host's environment—your carpet or drapes. Eggs are laid on the host, but also fall off to mature in the environment. The eggs may hatch promptly, or may not hatch for up to a year if the temperature and humidity in the environment are inhospitable. While the eggs are in their cocoon, *nothing* can harm them. They are impervious to pesticides, cold, drought, or floods. Their only weakness is that they can be vacuumed up and discarded in the vacuum bag.

A flea bite stings, but it can also cause *flea allergy dermatitis*—the most common animal skin disease in the world.

Many creatures, especially dogs, have a hypersensitivity to the saliva fleas secrete into the skin as they suck blood. The dog actually reacts to the components in the saliva, which cause the red marks, swelling, and itching more than the bite. One bite can cause an allergic dog to scratch for up to a week.

Bites and other signs of flea infestation can usually be found on your dog's belly, between his hind legs, and around his tail. You might actually spot a flea on your dog. If you see any of these signs, you can assume that there are many more fleas both on your pet and in your home. Both the dog and its environment must be treated, and treated repeatedly since new eggs are likely to hatch even when existing fleas have been eliminated. Use products as directed, coordinating dips, rinses, and shampoos with household fogging, vacuuming, and drape cleaning. You may want to consult your veterinarian about some of the new flea preventives like Program, the "flea pill" that is administered orally and helps your pet repel fleas.

Ticks

Aside from the sores and anemia associated with large infestations of ticks, ticks may transmit several diseases. Lyme disease is caused by the tiny deer tick. The symptoms in humans include a red rash surrounding the tick bite and flulike symptoms. In dogs, loss of appetite, fatigue, swollen glands, and lameness are the typical symptoms. If not diagnosed and treated promptly with antibiotics, Lyme disease can cause arthritis, impair the nervous system, and lead to heart or kidney disorders.

Rocky Mountain spotted fever is spread by the Rocky Mountain wood tick and by the American dog tick. Symptoms include a fever as high as 105 degrees, loss of appetite, coughing or labored breathing, and neurological impairment.

You should check your dog for ticks every day during the warm season. Ticks love to go where the dog's fur is thinner—especially around the ears and behind the elbows—but I have found ticks on every part of my dogs' anatomy, from the eyelids to the underbelly. When you find one, grasp it firmly as close to the skin as possible with tweezers. Turn the tick counterclockwise to unscrew it as you gently pull. You do not want to rip the head off and leave it embedded in your dog's flesh, so be careful. When it is out of your dog, you can drown the tick in alcohol to kill it.

Even if you remove the tick cleanly, you will notice a swollen spot on your pet in the days following. This swelling may form a small, hard lump with a scab on your dog's skin, which will eventually go away.

There are sprays and shampoos to combat ticks. As with flea control, you should use these under the advice of your veterinarian and follow the directions explicitly. As good as these products are, nothing is as effective as manually checking your dog every day.

What Is Normal for Your Dog?

Canines have a different heart rate, body temperature, and other signs of "health" than humans do. Before you can look

for problems, you need to know what is normal for your pet. Each individual has his or her unique activity level, sleep needs, appetite, and demeanor. But let's look at what is generally considered normal for a dog.

Temperature

A dog's normal body temperature can vary, from between 100 to 102.5 degrees Fahrenheit. Smaller dogs usually have temperatures in the higher range. The standard method of taking a dog's temperature is by rectal thermometer.

Taking Your Dog's Temperature

Have your dog lie on his side. Lubricate the tip of a shaken-down rectal thermometer with a little Vaseline and insert it gently into your dog's rectum at the appropriate angle. Don't put more than one inch of the thermometer into your dog. Talk gently to him and feed him treats to distract him and keep him quiet. Hold the end of the thermometer in case your pet moves. Keep the thermometer in place for three minutes and then remove it to read the result.

Pulse

Your dog's heart rate can vary from a resting 60 beats per minute to an active 150 beats per minute. The two main places to feel your dog's pulse are over his heart and from the femoral artery in each hind leg. Check your dog's pulse by running your hands down either side of his body behind his shoulders until your fingers touch under his chest, behind his elbows. You should feel the heart beating, strong and regular. You can also have your pet lie down on his side and run your hand up along the inside of his lower hind leg until you almost reach the belly. In male dogs, this spot will be below the scrotum. Press down gently and feel around until you find the pulsing femoral artery.

Mouth

The gums and underside of the lips in your dog's mouth should be pink in color. Even dogs like black chows who have black gums and a black tongue usually have little spots of pink that you can check. Changes in these membranes can indicate low oxygen levels or low red blood cell counts in your dog, and a veterinarian should be consulted. Become familiar with your dog's normal color. Pale pink, gray, bluish, or white lips and gums can spell trouble.

Water Consumption

This varies from dog to dog, but you should make a mental note of what your pet normally consumes. Serena drinks about one liter of water every thirty-six hours in the fall and winter. In the spring and summer, she consumes nearly one and a half liters a day. What about your pet?

Skin Pliability

A dog's skin can alert you to signs of dehydration. Gently lift a fold of your pet's skin and then release it. A healthy dog's skin will fall immediately back into its normal position. If the dog is dehydrated, the skin will stay in the fold position, then slowly return to normal. Contact your veterinarian if this happens.

Nose

The nose should be smooth, coolish—not necessarily cold—and without discharge. If a dog becomes warm, when sitting in a sunny car, for instance, his nose will feel warm as well. Dogs sneeze as we do when their nasal passages are irritated from inhaling some allergen or irritant.

Body Composition

Your dog should feel well muscled when you run your hands over her. Swelling, heat in areas, and tenderness or soreness indicate some trauma or other problem that should be attended to.

Movement

Your dog's movement should be free and easy. He should carry his weight evenly on each leg and paw. Any sign of favoring one leg or shortening a stride indicates lameness.

Signs That Your Pet May Be Ill

Dogs, like people, have their good days and their bad. They step on glass and pick up colds, viruses, and flus. This overview will give you an idea of what symptoms are *not* normal for your pet.

Appearance: A change in your dog's energy level, resulting in lethargy; weakness or loss of balance; unresponsiveness; and loss of consciousness. Marked weight loss or weight gain.

Eyes: Squinting or pawing at eyes; yellow or thick discharge; keeping the eyes closed; a red or yellow color in the white of the eye; pupils of different sizes; blindness.

Ears: Scratching at ears; holding them at a funny angle; shaking the head; a foul odor; any discharge; a hot, painful area; bloody discharge.

Nose: Nosebleeds; a cloudy or yellow discharge; dryness or cracking of the skin.

Mouth: Bleeding gums (unless he has just been chewing a stick and is all right); gray, white, or pale gums; an inability to fully open or close the mouth; a bad odor from the mouth. Tartar or plaque on teeth, broken teeth, or an unwillingness to eat are also signs that your veterinarian should be made aware of.

Heart and lungs: Irregular, labored, or difficult breathing; continuous panting when not exercising; excited or warm; frequent coughing, gagging, choking, or fainting.

Stomach and intestinal tract: Vomiting; diarrhea; loose, black, or bloody stools; consuming more or less water than normal; a sudden "ballooning" of the abdomen; a tucked-up, "crampy" appearance.

Urinary and genital areas: Bad-smelling or bloody urine.

- Females—discharge from the vulva (unless in heat or following whelping); masses or lumps in the breast tissue; bloody or smelly discharge from nipples.

- Males—unequal size of testicals; blood from penis.

- Both—straining to urinate; puddles of urine left where resting; increase or decrease in frequency of urination.

Skin: Continuous scratching or licking; crusty or scabby skin; wet sores that do not heal; a jaundiced color; hair loss.

Common Emergencies

Poisoning

Our human world is very toxic to our pets. From household cleaning products to antifreeze, rat poison, and baker's chocolate, there are many dangerous substances lurking around your home that your pet might ingest. Some of the signs of poisoning include tremors, muscle twitching, and convulsions; labored or shallow breathing; excessive salivation; vomiting or diarrhea; a tucked-up, crampy appearance; an abdomen sensitive to touch.

If you think that your dog has ingested something toxic, get him to the vet. Wrap him in a blanket in case he goes into shock. Bring the substance he ingested, and any vomit he may have produced, for the vet to inspect.

If you cannot get to your vet, call the **Pet Poison Hotline, 800-548-2423,** run by the National Animal Poison Control Center at the University of Illinois School of Veterinary Medicine. They should instruct you on how to proceed.

Burns

Surface burns happen to dogs quite frequently. Serena got a terrible one when she stuck her head under my mother's arm as Mom took a Thanksgiving turkey out of the oven. The pan tipped and a stream of scalding turkey grease spilled on Serena's ear. I grabbed wet towels and wiped the grease off her, but a tiny patch of fur had been burned off. We packed it

Canine Chocoholics Beware!

Although many of us just can't get enough of the tasty stuff, eating chocolate is extremely dangerous for your dog. Chocolate contains theobromine, which, when ingested by dogs in toxic doses, causes no end of problems, from vomiting and diarrhea to seizures, coma, and death. The amount of toxicity varies, depending on the strength of the chocolate and the size of the dog. Baker's chocolate, which is commonly used for cooking, is the most toxic. Ingesting as little as eight ounces can kill a sixty-pound dog. Milk chocolate is less toxic but still dangerous. If you find that your dog has ingested chocolate, call your veterinarian or the Animal Poison Control Center.

It's best simply to keep chocolate away from dogs altogether, despite the drooling and big, sad eyes you'll get from your canine chocoholic.

in ice and, under veterinary supervision, treated it with antibiotic ointment. It healed very well, but she still has a tiny, hairless spot on her ear from the burn. In general, you should cover the burn with cold, wet towels and take the dog to the vet. Large burns may need to be repaired with skin grafts. If you find a burn on your dog's lips or mouth, he has probably been chewing electrical cords and should be seen by a vet as soon as possible. Aside from the burn, he may have internal damage from the electric shock.

Seizures or Convulsions

Dogs have convulsions for a number of reasons, from poisoning or inherited epilepsy to liver or kidney disease. While dogs rarely die during these episodes, they are very scary to see. A dog may appear to be perfectly fine before and after the seizure, but should be seen by a veterinarian so that the cause of the fits can be treated.

A convulsing dog will not swallow his tongue, as a person will, so do not put your hand in the dog's mouth to seize it. You may be badly bitten. Wrap your pet in a blanket to contain the fits and prevent him from hurting himself.

Airway Obstructions

Dogs frequently get balls, pieces of sticks, and children's toys stuck behind their back teeth, blocking their breathing.

Giving Your Dog the Heimlich Maneuver

If your dog is still conscious and standing, get behind him and wrap your arms around his abdomen, bringing them together in a fist where the rib cage ends. Jerk up and in with your fist, toward the front of your pet. Keep trying if the object does not pop out. You can also try thumping both sides of the ribs with cupped hands.

If this does not work and your dog loses consciousness, extend his head and neck forward and open his mouth as widely as you can, pulling the tongue forward, out of the way. Look for the object at the back of his throat and put your fingers in as far back as you can to try and pull it out. Take your pet to the veterinarian for an examination to be sure he has no other damage.

You will see them opening their mouths wide, trying desperately to breathe. If you can, hold your pet's jaws apart and dislodge the object with your fingers.

If you can't reach the stick or ball, you may need to perform a modified Heimlich maneuver on your pet.

Drowning

Water safety is very important for your pet. Teach pups to swim to the ladder to exit a pool, do not leave dogs unsupervised by backyard pools, and make them wear a life preserver when swimming. Hundreds of dogs drown every year in their own backyards, so prevent this emergency.

If you find your dog drowning, get him out of the water and check to see if he is breathing and what color his gums are. If they are blue or ashen gray, he lacks oxygen. Lift the dog's hind end up to tip his head down, and thump his sides to try and drain the water out of him. You may not get very much water out since it will have forced its way down into his airway. Take him to the veterinarian immediately.

Bloat and Gastric Torsion

Bloat is a deadly stomach disorder that affects mainly the large, deep-chested breeds and occasionally medium and small breeds. Bloat frequently occurs after a meal, after physical activity, or during a period of stress, but the precise cause is unknown.

If your dog is bloating, he will suddenly look blown up, as though his stomach and sides were full of air. He may try to vomit with little success, salivate, or look depressed and uncomfortable. His stomach has twisted around so that it cannot empty either by vomiting or burping. The process is extremely painful, as the stomach fills with fluid and gas, blowing up like a balloon. The twisting and bloating interrupt blood flow from the heart to the stomach tissue and spleen. Complications from the death of the stomach and spleen kill the dog.

If you notice any bloaty symptoms in your pet, take him immediately to the nearest veterinary hospital. Without prompt surgical intervention, your dog will soon go into shock and will die. Even with prompt veterinary care, mortality rates from bloat can be as high as 60 percent.

No one is exactly sure why dogs bloat, but there are several studies trying to find clues. Increased risk of bloat seems to be age related—dogs seven years or older are twice as likely to bloat as two- to four-year-olds. Purebreds are three times as likely to bloat as mixed breeds. You should memorize the warning signs of bloat, and be wary. I always keep a watchful eye on Serena, particularly when there is a lot of stress in our life. Only by close observation and quick action can you save your pet.

Heat Exhaustion and Heatstroke

Dogs are quite susceptible to heat exhaustion and heatstroke since they cannot perspire as we can.

Heat exhaustion comes about after exercise—usually in hot or humid weather. Heatstroke happens when the dog's internal body temperature goes up because the dog is left in a hot car or other unbearably warm environment.

In either case, the dog may vomit, breathe rapidly, or collapse, or experience tremors and faint. You need to cool the

All RAWHIDE Is Not Created Equal!

Does your dog love to chew on rawhide? Do you indulge him in knots and rings, thinking that he's safe gnawing on the leather? Think again. The only rawhide that is safe for dogs to chew on—and ingest—is the very thickest, whitest rawhide made from hides tanned in the United States. Here, strict guidelines govern anything produced to be ingested by humans or animals, so hides for use in rawhide chews are free of chemicals or poisonous elements like lead and arsenic compounds. They are also thicker or of a heavier weight. Only very heavy rawhide has the fiber to pass cleanly through your dog's system. Thin, cheaply tanned leather can become slimy and stick in your dog's digestive system, where digestive enzymes may leach harmful chemicals from the leather. Only buy heavy, white, U.S.-made rawhide. When you see the thin brownish-yellow stuff in the supermarket, walk on by.

pet's entire body with cool water, not iced, and put a fan on the pet to aid evaporation. If the dog's rectal temperature is 105 degrees or higher, immerse the pet's entire body, except his head, in cold water as quickly as possible.

This is a real problem for dogs left in parked cars, and for this reason, several states have passed laws prohibiting owners from leaving pets alone in vehicles.

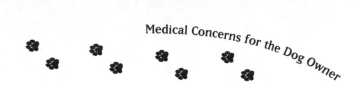
Bee Stings and Skunk "Encounters"

Bee stings can cause a dangerous allergic reaction in dogs. If you think that your dog was stung by a bee, and she is having difficulty breathing, call your veterinarian. If she seems fine but the bee sting is sore, squeeze some fresh aloe vera gel, or put some mud, on the spot. Continue to observe your pet for signs of an allergic reaction.

If your dog has the misfortune of getting "skunked," you can clean him up with:

Mix:

> 1 quart hydrogen peroxide (drugstore type)
> 1/4 cup baking soda
> 1 tablespoon liquid soap

Douse the dog with this mixture without getting it too close to his eyes. Follow with a thorough water rinse.

Alternative Therapies

Alternative therapies, like homeopathy, herbal treatments, and acupuncture, offer a different approach to wellness. Many veterinarians providing these treatments have a foundation in conventional medicine, and mix the therapies. These alternative veterinarians report startling successes with various canine health disorders, from chronic ailments to incurable, progressive conditions like arthritis.

How to Give Your Dog a Pill

The easy way to trick your pet into taking his pills is just to wrap them in hamburger or butter and toss them to him. Toss him a few chunks without pills to get him in the rhythm, then sneak in the pill. If he won't take his pills as treats, you'll have to resort to giving them to him manually. Hold his mouth open, place the pill on the back of his tongue, and close his mouth. Hold his jaws shut and gently massage his throat until he swallows.

Your Canine First-Aid Kit

In case of emergency, and to be able to offer prompt aid to your pet, you should have these things handy in your home:

—a rectal thermometer

—gauze, cotton pads, and surgical tape

—Quick-Stop or a styptic pencil to quell bleeding

—activated charcoal and milk of magnesia for poison antidotes

—Betadine antiseptic solution and ointment

Perhaps you feel that your veterinarian has exhausted the regular treatments for your dog's symptoms, and you're ready

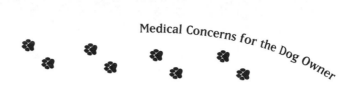

to try something different. Whatever your reason for turning to alternative therapies, there are excellent veterinarians to guide you.

Keep the Human Medicine Cabinet Closed to Dogs

You should never administer common human medications, like aspirin, to your pet without veterinary supervision. Human-strength dosages of pain relievers like ibuprofen (Advil), aspirin, and especially acetaminophen (Tylenol) can give dogs severe and painful stomach ulcers. So if your pet seems sore after a long jog, call your veterinarian for a quick consultation before you simply toss him a pain reliever.

Veterinary Acupuncture

This involves the stimulation of various points on the body, causing biochemical and physiological changes. Acupuncture increases circulation, relieves pain by releasing many neurotransmitters, including the body's own natural painkillers—endorphins—and stimulates the body's defense system. Acupuncture has been used successfully for over 4,000 years on animals as well as humans, and is considered one of the safest therapies when performed by a competent acupuncturist. In dogs, acupuncture is commonly used to treat musculoskeletal problems like hip dysplasia, arthritis, disk disease,

and long-term injuries, as well as skin and respiratory problems, traumatic nerve injuries, and even epilepsy.

You can get more information about veterinary acupuncture from the International Veterinary Acupuncture Society, P.O. Box 2074, Nederland, CO 80466, 303-258-3767, and the Center for Veterinary Acupuncture, 1405 West Silver Spring Drive, Glendale, WI 53209, 414-352-0201.

Homeopathy

Homeopathy is a system of medicine that works by stimulating an individual's "healing energies" through carefully matched, nontoxic remedies. Prepared from plant, mineral, and animal substances, the entire system of remedies is natural. If you are interested in learning about homeopathic treatments for your pets, you can get more information from the **American Veterinary Holistic Medical Association,** 2214 Old Emmorton Road, Bel Air, MD 21015, 410-569-0795, or visit their Web page, ALTVETMED: http://www.monmouth.com/~altvetmed.

An excellent book to begin with is *Dr. Pitcairn's Complete Guide to Natural Health for Dogs and Cats* by Richard Pitcairn, DVM, and Susan Hubble Pitcairn (Rodale Press). It outlines a natural approach to animal husbandry, from pet food recipes to drug-free, holistic treatments for common animal disorders.

Other great resources are *The Natural Rearing Newsletter*, P.O. Box 1436, Jacksonville, OR 97530, 503-899-2080, E-mail: AMBRICAM@cdsnet.net and the catalogue of

Your Smoking and Your Dog

In case you were looking for another reason to quit, you should be aware of the effects of your cigarette smoking on your dog. A study at Colorado State University's College of Veterinary Medicine and Biomedical Sciences showed that inhaling secondhand smoke can seriously damage a dog's health. Pets are as prone to cancers as humans are, and the study found that dogs with short or medium-length snouts whose owners smoke have a 50 percent greater risk of developing lung cancer.

Interestingly, longer-snouted breeds owned by smokers seem to have a normal risk of lung cancer, but are more susceptible to nasal cancer. Long- or short-nosed, all dogs are affected by the harmful irritants and carcinogens that are byproducts of smoking. Remember, your dog doesn't have a choice.

Whiskers Natural Pet Store, 235 East 9th Street, New York, NY 10003, 800-WHISKERS (944-7537).

Whatever approach you choose to take for your pet's health, your love and support when he is under the weather will make the greatest difference to him.

II

Your Rights and Responsibilities
*The Law and Your Dog, Canine Health
Insurance, and Protecting Your Pet from
Loss or Theft*

In May 1810, the Common Council of the bustling city of
New York created a new city office: the Office of Register and
Collector of Dogs. Along with the new office, a law was
passed requiring city dog owners to register and license their
pets for the sum of three dollars (a *lot* of money 185 years
ago!). Any dog found without a registration tag was to be
seized by the city and exterminated. A man named Abner
Curtis was hired as the first city dog collector, and he in turn
hired dogcatchers, offering them fifty cents for each untagged
dog they apprehended.

The law went into effect a month later, in June, but things

didn't go as smoothly as the Common Council, or Officer Curtis, had planned. On three separate occasions, when dog-catchers tried to take unlicensed dogs away, angry mobs of more than a hundred people quickly formed and stopped the dogs' apprehension, freeing the captured dogs and smashing the dogcatchers' carts. Because it was an expression of popular outrage, the crowds went unpunished. After several frustrating months, during which only a very few dogs were successfully seized without civic unrest, the council and Officer Curtis abandoned their attempt to clear the city of unregistered canines. However, laws governing dogs in New York or other cities and towns in the United States did not go away.

So where do canines stand today?

Legal Requirements

Most states and municipalities require that dogs be vaccinated against rabies and licensed with the town clerk's office, animal control, or the health department. Once your dog is licensed, he must wear a tag with his registration number, as well as his rabies tag, on his collar at all times.

Most states also have anti-roaming statutes, making it illegal for owners to allow their dogs to run at liberty. Of course, roaming dogs are in constant danger from cars. But in rural areas, if dogs are allowed to roam, even the sweetest pet can become a "sport hunter" when his prey drive kicks in, chasing and killing other domestic animals or livestock like rabbits, chicken, and sheep.

In addition to anti-roaming statutes, towns and municipalities frequently also have leash laws. These require dog owners to restrain their pets on a leash when off their property, or in a public area like a park.

Frequently, cities like New York also require you to pick up and dispose of your pet's waste. Some counties have zoning ordinances dictating how many dogs you can own, or requiring a kennel license for keeping more than three adult dogs on a property or dictating minimum acreage requirements for kennels.

Wherever you live you should make a quick phone call to the town clerk's office, zoning office, or animal control officer to find out which local laws govern your pet.

Housing Problems

The housing outlook for dog owners can be difficult. Many rental leases prohibit pets. You may have to look long and hard to find an apartment that will accept your dog, or you may have to pay a hefty "pet deposit," but it's not impossible.

If you have your heart set on a place that does not allow dogs, it is worth trying to convince a reluctant landlord. Make sure that your pet is calm, well mannered, and will do a down-stay on command. Work with a trainer to prep for this if necessary. Make an appointment to meet the landlord, and use the opportunity to demonstrate how well behaved your pet is. Sometimes the rules can be "bent" for a friendly dog

who lies quietly by her master's side during the interview, impressing the landlord with her manners.

New York City's huge rental market had so many cases of landlords evicting tenants because of their dogs that legislation was necessary. New York City's Administrative Code, section 27-2009.1, or the "three-month law," applies to all rent-regulated apartments, co-ops, and condos in buildings with three or more units.

Simply put, even if your lease reads "No Dogs Allowed," if you get a dog and keep her in your apartment without trying to conceal her presence, the landlord, or governing body of the building, has three months in which to formally act against you. They *must* bring a lawsuit. Threatening phone calls or a letter don't count. If the landlord fails to sue within the three-month period, the "no dogs" part of your lease becomes void, and you can legally keep your pet. Even better, any dogs you get after the initial "lease-breaker dog" are "grandfathered" in, meaning that you can continue to keep dogs in the apartment.

Nuisance Complaints

The most common cause of problems for dog owners are nuisance complaints filed by landlords or neighbors. A "nuisance" would be a dog who menaced the neighbors, continually barked, or an owner with many, many pets in too small an area. However, the burden of proof is on the person who complains—landlord or neighbor—to establish that your pet, or pets, are causing a problem. A "nuisance" is a flexible stan-

dard subject to interpretation. Isolated instances of barking, for example, cannot be considered a consistent nuisance.

If there are complaints against your dog, the animal control officers in your area will act as mediators between you and the complainant to resolve the dispute. The best thing you can do in this situation is to impress the officers with how well mannered and under control your dogs are. If animal control considers you to be a responsible owner, you have a distinct advantage.

Dangerous Dogs

Of course we want our dogs to protect us. If a burglar breaks into my apartment or a fake deliveryman tries to force his way through my door in the middle of the day, I expect my German shepherd to stop them. But what if she *misjudges* a situation, grabbing the real UPS man or a neighborhood child who shows up unexpectedly on the back stoop? If your dog nips an innocent person instead of a threatening person, *you and your dog* could be in serious trouble.

What happens in a dog-bite case depends on the severity of the incident. Typically, the bitee reports the incident to the local police or dog warden. The officers interview the people on both sides about the incident and make a judgment. If it's a severe bite, there's not much discussion. Your dog will be quarantined for at least two weeks in a boarding facility, at your expense, or will be put in "protective custody" at a canine control facility in your area.

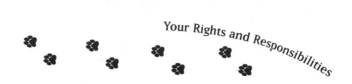

In some states a hearing follows in which a hearing officer or judge decides your dog's fate. In others, the dog warden makes the decision. If you disagree with the warden's decision, you usually have the right to a hearing in front of a judge. In this situation, you certainly should consult a lawyer. Besides wanting to get your dog back, you might be facing a tort liability lawsuit for damages, since the chances are excellent that your dog's victim is physically or mentally scarred in some way.

Liability insurance for dog bites is generally covered under your blanket home owner's or renter's insurance. But most lawyers who have handled these cases say that dog owners should check their policies. Lawyers recommend insurance for between $1 and $3 million in liability.

In these instances, animal control officers and courts can be "breed prejudiced," meaning that if your dog looks anything like a pit bull, Doberman, rottweiler, or German shepherd, there is a greater assumption of guilt. Your lawyer will handle things, but you may need expert witnesses, animal behaviorists, and dog trainers to testify in defense of your pet.

In the best-case scenario, the hearing officer or judge finds your dog's aggression understandable and warranted, and you are found not liable for any damages. Following the quarantine period, your life returns to normal. Your home owner's policy absorbs the victim's bill and their "pain and suffering" lawsuit. You and your dog go your way, older and wiser.

If things don't go so well, the warden or judge may determine that your dog is a "dangerous dog" and order you to do any number of things to keep your pet: register your dog as "dangerous" with the municipality; muzzle or confine him; take out special liability insurance; or complete a course of obedience or anti-bite training. The judge may also order the dog removed from the area (your dog gets to live, just not there) or destroyed. This may be accompanied by a liability verdict for more money than your insurance can pay—or you may not have insurance. In addition to losing your dog, you could face severe financial problems.

There is a common belief that "the first bite is a freebie," meaning that if a dog has absolutely no history of unprovoked aggression, the owner should not be held responsible. This is not necessarily true. Liability for dog bites only requires a showing of negligence on the part of the dog owner, or that the owner did not exercise reasonable care. For instance, if your dog bites someone when he is off the leash in a leash-law area, you are already at fault.

People love to sue. We live in a world of million-dollar legal settlements. Once your dog bites someone, often even if the attack was provoked, you are liable. Lawsuits have been filed *and won* by people who were bitten after poking their fingers, or sticks, through chain-link fences to tease dogs. A "Beware of Dog" sign does not shield you in any way from tort liability.

The moral of the story is: PROTECT YOURSELF AND YOUR DOG! We ask a lot of dogs living in our society: to learn our customs, to communicate with us, and *sometimes* to distinguish between members of our own species. We expect a

dog to recognize the difference between a "good person" and an "evildoer," something *we often can't do ourselves.*

Don't ask your pet to make distinctions between people. If he's the least bit aggressive to strangers, put him in another room when you let the deliveryman in. Don't force him to tolerate children, and if your child has friends over, don't leave them unsupervised with your pet. If you have any question about how your dog might react to a situation, put him in his crate or in another room. DON'T GIVE YOUR DOG THE CHANCE TO BITE SOMEONE. If he does, you both lose.

Your Dog's Effect on Your Home Insurance

As I mentioned, dogs are usually covered by your home owner's or renter's insurance. Unfortunately, the breed or number of dogs you own can decide whether or not a company will cover you.

Insurance companies have begun to prevent potentially expensive claims by simply denying coverage to dog owners of "dangerous" breeds. Even one dog-bite claim against your pet will cost the insurance company thousands of dollars, so they have become very wary. Dog breeds especially targeted are all the protection breeds, chows, and any dog who remotely resembles a pit bull. Companies consider these dogs to present a significant risk factor.

As unjust as it sounds, company decisions are often based only on breed stereotypes, not on the temperament of the individual dog. But since each insurance company can make

up its own guidelines for coverage, it is well within their right to try and minimize their liability.

If you are denied insurance by a company, there are things you can do to fight back:

- Chronicle that your dog has never been aggressive by showing a clean record with the local animal control office. Show Canine Good Citizen awards and obedience school certificates, and get statements from your neighbors, veterinarian, and dog trainer testifying to the fact that your dog is a sweetie.

- Show that your dog is appropriately housed in a secure run, or that your property is completely fenced in.

- Invite the agent to inspect your property and meet your dog.

- Try different companies.

Canine Health Insurance

If your pet has a serious illness or accident, a major chunk of change can evaporate—and you certainly don't want to be in the position of denying your dog medical services because of money. To soften a potential financial blow, several companies offer pet health insurance. Just like human insurance, there is a membership fee, a choice of deductibles, a maximum amount they will pay per year and per illness, and some

perks for joining. Of course, there are limitations. The list of potential health problems excluded from coverage is significant and includes maladies like hip or elbow dysplasia, which are genetically passed, and any illness your pet should have been vaccinated against. However, if your dog is hit by a car, has some other accident, or is diagnosed with cancer, this plan can really help. For more information contact **Veterinary Pet Insurance,** DVM Insurance Agency, 4175 La Palma Avenue #100, Anaheim, CA 92807, 800-USA-PETS.

When Your Dog Is Lost or Stolen

Obviously, the best cure for this is prevention. *DO NOT* let your dog roam. *DO NOT* leave him outside alone, unless in a secure run. Networks of pet thieves and dealers who make a tidy profit supplying stolen pet dogs (and cats) to laboratories have been well documented, most comprehensively in Judith Reitman's book, *Stolen for Profit: How the Biomedical Industry Is Funding a National Pet Theft Conspiracy* (Pharos/St. Martin Press, 1993; available in bookstores, or through **In Defense of Animals,** 816 West Francisco Boulevard, San Rafael, CA 94901, 415-453-9984).

Cities and residential suburbs are favorite targets of dog-theft rings because of the concentrated numbers of dogs and their availability. At one point, 10,000 dogs disappeared from the Rochester, New York, area in a six-month period! How many dogs have you seen tied in backyards, or roaming around a neighborhood? Each one is a potential victim. Please

take every precaution with your dog to protect him from theft.

Dogs also just get lost. If the unthinkable happens to your pet, there are some things you can do to improve your chances of getting her back. Membership in one of the several organizations and registry services who offer lost/stolen pet protection is a great start. The more you do to make your dog easily identifiable, the better your chances of preventing theft and getting her back if she gets lost.

If your pet is lost, contact your local humane society, animal control officers, and veterinarians. Blanket your area with signs, including a photo of your pet. You can also contact **800-STOLEN-PET**, the hot line of In Defense of Animals, and **PETFINDERS**, at 800-666-5678. These nonprofit organizations will counsel owners who have lost their dogs.

Stay focused and positive about recovery and work like mad to find your dog. Your determination and effort may make the difference!

PREVENTION: TATTOO YOU

The most popular way to permanently identify a dog is by tattoo—no, not the motto "Born to Chew" over a bone. An ID/registration number from a dog registry organization is inconspicuously and painlessly tattooed on your dog's belly or inner hind leg. With this lasting means of identification, it is much easier to locate him or her in a shelter or pound, and it may save his life if he is stolen for laboratory use.

If thieves have taken your dog, a tattoo is the only thing

that can save him. Laboratories will not accept tattooed dogs from the dealers the thieves supply. It is important to tattoo your dog on the belly or inner thigh, not inside his ear. Thieves have been known to *cut* the tattooed portion of the dog's ear off to prevent identification.

Tattoo registries keep their records permanently, and continue to actively search for your dog. **Tattoo-A-Pet,** 1625 Emmons Avenue, Brooklyn, NY 11235, 800-TATTOOS, the **National Dog Registry,** 800-NDR-DOGS, and Identipet, 800-243-9147 register and tattoo companion animals.

MICROCHIPPING

Microchipping dogs for identification is the newest way to have your pet identified. It involves a veterinarian implanting a transponder microchip, about the size of a grain of rice, underneath the skin on your dog's shoulder blades. The chip is programmed with a code number, and gives off a signal at a specific radio frequency. When scanned with a compatible scanner, all the information identifying your pet pops up on a computer screen.

The overwhelming problem with microchipping right now is that there are several companies selling chips and scanners, and some of them are not compatible. So if your dog finds his way to a shelter with a scanner from company A, and the chip you implanted in your dog is from company B, your dog is out of luck. Also, since the chip is not visible, the way a tattoo is, it offers no protection from pet theft.

Companies are working toward industry cohesion, so microchipping is a good idea, but you might want to play it safe and still get your dog tattooed.

You can get more information on microchips from:

HomeAgain, 800-252-7894; fax 919-233-1290 or E-mail: found@AKC.org.

InfoPet, 800-INFOPET; fax 612-890-2054

Who Will Take Care of Your Dog in Your Absence?

An issue too frequently overlooked is what will happen to your pet if *you* become ill or pass away. As a concerned, responsible dog owner, you need to consider this question and make arrangements if necessary so that he will be cared for as you would want him to be.

Most of us do not want to think about this scenario, but we probably should. If you are lucky enough to have a partner, friend, or family member who will keep your dog, then you have nothing to worry about. If you are not so sure, you might want to make some arrangements ahead of time. **Alpha Affiliates,** 103 Washington Street, Suite 362, Morristown, NJ 07960, 201-539-2770, will provide you with durable power of attorney for pet care. The document offers guidance and the means to authorize care for your pets should you be unable to do so. You will be asked to name a specific agent, as well as a backup, who will be responsible for your pets. You

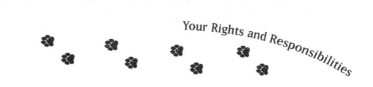

will also need to make financial provisions in your estate for your pet's continuing care. The document itself can be used, or it can serve as a model for a section you may want added to your will.

Many humane societies and private shelters offer "Surviving Pet Care Programs." When your pet is enrolled in one of them, the organization will assume custody of him when you are gone, care for him, and find him a permanent new home. Usually there is no minimum charge for your pet to join, but since the shelters are supported by contribution, acceptance into such a program *should certainly* be followed by a bequest if at all possible.

To prepare, have your attorney clearly specify in your will that you wish your animals to be given to the shelter. Because wills are sometimes not read until a few weeks after death, the organizations suggest that you restate the information in a letter of intent, and leave it with a friend or relative who can call the shelter immediately so that your dog doesn't languish, alone and uncared for, in your home. Including up-to-date medical records and information on your pet's temperament and preferences will ensure that he gets the best continuing care.

Dog ownership is no longer as simple as it may have been when a pup followed you home from school one day and your mom let you keep him as long as he stayed on the porch. Today, owning a pet brings serious legal and financial consequences. Please, do everything you can to be a model dog owner.

A Life Together

Daily Upkeep, Traveling with Your Pet,
Pet-Sitters, and Boarding Kennels

The life you spend with your pet encompasses years together. Here are suggestions for giving him the best care possible, every day, at home or as you explore the world by traveling together.

Daily Feedings

Creatures of habit, dogs thrive on a predictable schedule. Puppies should receive three meals each day until eight months or one year of age, and older dogs two meals per day. When they are fed two small meals rather than a single huge

one, dogs are less worried about food since they don't have long periods of hunger. Also, it is much easier for them to digest two smaller meals instead of one huge one. By eating in the morning and early evening, your dog benefits from an adequate and consistent level of blood sugar during his waking hours. He also has time to digest and evacuate before bedtime.

It is not a good idea to leave your dog's food available to him at all times. "Free feeding" is a very unnatural situation for canines and it encourages bad eating habits. When food is available all day, dogs either become gluttonous and gain weight or they become finicky.

Never overlook the symbolic power that food represents to your canine. In the wild, food is survival. Within wolf packs the leaders, who are also the best hunters, possess the killed prey and decide in which order other pack members may partake of it. Lower-ranking members know that they must obey the pack leaders to earn the privilege of sharing the food.

The same is true in your home. Dogs know that food is power. As pack leader, you must control it. Leaving dry food available all day for your pet gives him the power.

Puppy or adult dog, the best approach is to prepare your pet's meal in his presence so that he gets to enjoy the production. Make him sit or lie down as he waits, thus "earning" the right to eat by obeying you. Put the food down and give him the "okay" command to start eating. Let him eat for fifteen minutes and then pick up the bowl. Most dogs eat quickly enough for that to be plenty of time. If your dog doesn't finish everything in that period, take up the bowl until the next feeding. Offer him his normal amount the next time, again giving him a time limit. This system confirms to your pet that you are in charge.

WHAT TO FEED YOUR DOG

Be sure that whatever food you select is designed for your dog's stage of life and activity level. Puppies need a puppy formula, with added calcium and protein for bone and cell development. Working dogs, show dogs under stress, and dogs who are underweight should receive a high-potency "performance" feed. Sedentary house dogs, older pets, or "gobblers"—dogs who inhale their meals and look expectantly for more—should get a low-potency "lite" or low-calorie feed that will allow them to eat enough to feel satisfied without adding extra pounds.

Select a dog food that lists a meat-, chicken-, or fish-based protein source as the first item in the ingredients. Avoid those that list corn, soybean, or animal meal as the main ingredient, or those that contain corn syrup.

You should avoid the controversial chemical preservatives ethoxyquin, BHA, and BHT as well.

I always wet my dogs' dry food with warm water and let it soak and expand for a few minutes before I feed them. Dry food can really blow up, and I want that to happen before it goes in my dog's stomach.

Although vegetarians and proponents of an all-dry-food

diet will disagree with me, I also feed my dogs raw meat. Raw beef, chicken, and organ meats, in particular, contain not only all the amino acids your dog needs, but live enzymes that aid in digestion. I buy frozen mixed organ meats, but you can also get raw meat from a meat packer or a butcher. In a pinch, I just buy frozen hamburger and add about half a cup to Serena's daily meals.

Consult your veterinarian for exact advice on how much to feed your dog. I have found the guidelines printed on dog food labels to be very misleading. They often exaggerate how much food is necessary to sustain a pet in top form.

HOMEMADE DOG BISCUITS

> 1 cup whole wheat flour
> 1 cup white flour
> 1/2 cup powdered milk
> 2/3 stick margarine
> 1 egg
> 1/3 cup water
> 1 teaspoon brown sugar
> 1 jar baby food meat

Combine all ingredients. Mix and knead well. Roll out on a cookie sheet, and cut into bone shapes with a knife or cookie cutter. Bake at 325 degrees for thirty minutes. Allow to cool in oven. Makes two dozen biscuits.

Grooming Your Pet

My friend Ruth always jokes that her idea of grooming dogs is to throw a stick in a pond. But jokes aside, all dogs need "hygienic upkeep." Even breeds that don't require clips and trims must have their toenails, matted hair, and dirty ears attended to.

Depending on the breed, it is not difficult to keep your pet well groomed. A daily brushing makes the difference between a kempt and an unkempt pet. It also leaves your dog feeling loved and cared for. Be sure to brush sensitive areas gently: Never bear down too hard. If your vet shows you how, you can keep on top of toenails and dirty ears as well, and baths and flea dips can be done in your tub or the backyard.

EARS AND TOES

You can safely clean your dog's ears, and keep his toenails trimmed, at home. You may prefer not to do this, since one slip of the nail clippers can lead to bloodshed if you cut too close to the vein in your dog's nail. One nick with the nail trimmers can cause yelps of pain and reproachful looks from your pet for weeks to come. If you are still game, here are some ideas.

Ears

Dogs' ears accumulate dust and dirt and should be swabbed out. Armed with a pile of treats, have your dog sit in front of you. Moisten a tissue or some cotton with water (just moist—not dripping wet) or an ear-cleaning agent from your vet or a pet-supply store. Gently rub the dirt off the ear flap and give your dog a treat. Moisten another tissue and wrap it around your index finger. Gently sweep your wrapped finger around the base of the ear without probing deeply. This may feel good to your dog and he may lean into you or give a low, grumbly sound of pleasure. Give your dog another treat for good behavior and repeat if you still see dirt.

Praise your pet for cooperating with the ear cleaning. If he gets scared, or does not want you to touch his ears, that may indicate a painful ear infection that your vet should look at.

Toenails

Start with a pile of treats, Quick-Stop or a styptic pencil to stop bleeding, and sharp canine nail clippers. Do not use human clippers unless your dog has tiny nails, and get heavy-duty clippers if you have a large dog with thick nails.

Have your dog sit in front of you and give him a treat. Take one front paw, separate one toe, and quickly nip off the very tip of the nail. Let the paw go, praise him, and give him another treat. If that was successful, pick up the other front paw, separate another toe, and snip one on that side. Release the paw, praise him, and give him another treat. Stop for the day. Do the same thing the next day, only cutting one or two toes each day with much praise and many treats. Continue the routine until all toes, front and back, are done.

If you attempt to clip an entire paw in one sitting, your dog may become uncomfortable and not hold still. By doing only one or two toes a day, you will ensure that nail clipping will be safe and not frightening to your pet.

YOUR CANINE'S CANINES

As silly as it sounds, you should brush your dog's teeth every day. Like those of humans, a dog's teeth are subject to periodontal disease and decay. But don't read this and grab the tube of Crest. You'll need doggie toothpaste, which doesn't foam and tastes like the flavors dogs *want* in their mouths—chicken or liver. You can buy a kit containing paste, a toothbrush, and a few "dental wipes"—breath-freshening tissues—to rub over your dog's teeth.

Unless you've been brushing your canine's canines since his puppyhood, this is going to come as a rude surprise to him. Go slowly. Start by rubbing your finger over his teeth and gums and move up to a finger with a little paste on it. If all goes well, next time you can introduce the brush. Serena never progressed to the brush. She hated it, so I got her a little "finger brush." This is a sort of extended plastic thimble with bristles, which works pretty well.

You can also buy dog toys that help clean teeth and freshen breath. **Dental Kong**, available in most pet-supply stores, is a dog toy that reduces plaque and helps reduce bad breath. Nylabone offers several dog-toy products that reduce plaque as your dog plays with them: Nylafloss, a knot of ham bone–flavored nylon, works in the same way your dental floss does, and Plaque Attacker has raised "dental tips" to get between teeth as your dog chews. Tooth decay and periodontal disease can cause problems that quickly become expensive for your veterinarian to fix. Brushing your dog's teeth daily is the easiest way to prevent these complications.

GROOMERS

Of course you might not want to deal with hefting that 120-pound Akita into your bathtub. At these times you can turn to a professional dog groomer. The hair artisans of the dog world, they magically turn our dirty, smelly canine companions back into bundles of love.

All dogs benefit from a trip to the groomer. Properly done, a grooming is a health benefit as well as an aesthetic treatment. In addition to bathing and styling the coat, groomers will trim the hair between your dog's paw pads, which can knot, causing a stone-in-shoe effect. They will clean the ears, genitals, and around the anus with a medicated solution and safely trim the toenails.

In addition to these basics, groomers offer many special treatments, from hot oil and sulphur baths for dogs with skin problems to antistatic treatments for their hair. Even anti-allergy washes can be applied to your dog's coat. These decrease the amount of dander he gives off, helping the allergic dog lovers in your home. Obviously, fleas and ticks are a concern, and your groomer can help you combat that yearly onslaught with effective, less toxic products than those you might commonly buy.

Finding a Groomer

When looking for a reputable groomer, keep several things in mind. A clean, well-run shop looks it. Things that should press your warning button are: an unpleasant smell, or the refusal to let you see the back area where the dogs are groomed. This does not mean that you should disrupt business by touring the room with a white glove, but a reputable place with nothing to hide should let you take a quick peek into the grooming area.

While waiting for their turn in the bathtub or on the grooming table, dogs are regularly kept in crates or wire cages. If you see any fecal matter or urine in a cage with a dog—lazy groomers may let a dog sit in a mess until it is their turn to be groomed—that would be a reason not to use the shop.

If you are a nonsmoker, make sure that the shop you send your dog to does not permit smoking on the premises; otherwise your expensively cleaned dog may come home smelling of cigarette smoke.

In general, if a grooming shop makes you feel the least bit uncomfortable, go elsewhere. You can get information about dog groomers in your area by contacting the **National Dog Groomers Association**, P.O. Box 101, Clark, PA 16113, 412-962-2711.

Some groomers offer to expel your dog's anal glands, something best left to your vet. These glands are small sacs on either side of the rectum, which inflate and deflate as they're expelled. When impacted, the glands don't deflate properly during the normal course of business and become uncomfortable. Dogs will try to alleviate the discomfort themselves by dragging their backsides along the ground. Only a veterinarian or trained vet tech should attempt to expel the glands.

Traveling with Your Pet

The relationship of complementary companions I hope you can build with your dog will take you many places together. The more you share, the deeper your connection will grow. This bond can lead the two of you to explore the world together as you enjoy traveling with your pet by your side.

So before you automatically call the pet-sitter or boarding kennel, why not consider taking your pet with you? Obviously, there are times when you must travel alone, but it *is* possible to take your dog on more trips and vacations than you might think. Extra planning and preparation are needed, but the rewards are great.

AIR TRAVEL

Nearly one thousand animals fly daily within the United States, but there are some things to be aware of to ensure a safe and stress-free flight for your dog.

After several gruesome incidents in which pets died while being shipped, the safety of air travel for animals has been contested in the press. The USDA estimates that between fifty and one hundred animals die in aircraft baggage compartments each year, mainly from suffocation or heatstroke. These deaths are frequently unreported, and airlines often record pet deaths as lost baggage.

Traveling during hot weather is the common denominator in most tragic stories. If you find yourself stuck on a hot runway with your dog in baggage, there is little you can do but hope for the best. Returning to the terminal to unload a dog would delay the flight's takeoff. The only way to avoid this situation is to schedule your flights from hot climates accordingly. Only fly very early in the morning, when you could afford to lose an hour or two before the heat hits, or late in the evening when the heat of the sun is gone. Ask what "equipment" or type of airplane is scheduled for your flight. Always try to fly on the largest, newest planes, because they have more space and better air-conditioning systems.

When you purchase your ticket, you will have to tell the airline that you plan to fly with your dog. They will reserve the space in either the baggage compartment or the main cabin if your canine pal is small enough to stay with you in the passenger cabin. There are usually limits as to how many dogs they can accommodate in either space, so make sure the information is in your flight record. If you decide to take your dog after you have purchased your tickets, call the airline immediately to inform them.

WHAT YOU'LL NEED

Federal law requires you to carry a current health certificate from your vet attesting to your dog's fitness and vaccinations when you travel between states by air or car. All foreign countries require their own documentation as well as a health certificate filled out usually no more then ten days before the flight. Other countries have their own import forms, available through their consulate, as well as customs clearance documents. Check with your airline or the capital of the state you are flying to, or call the consulate of the foreign country beforehand so that you have enough time to assemble the necessary paperwork.

To make all this a little easier, the **ASPCA** in New York puts out a booklet entitled "Traveling with Your Pet," listing the many safety concerns you should be aware of, as well as the documentation requirements for over 177 countries. To obtain a copy, send $5 to **The ASPCA Transportation Department, 424 East 92nd Street, New York, NY 10128.** If you have further questions, call the ASPCA at 212-876-7700, ext. 4402.

Mark your crate clearly with "LIVE ANIMAL" in big, bold letters, as well as arrows indicating which way is up, and a sign on the top with your dog's name, home address, and phone number, vacation destination address, and, most important, FLIGHT ITINERARY. Your dog is much more likely to be loaded on the correct flight if there is a big sign on his crate *reminding* the baggage folks to load him.

For the Small Dogs in the Audience

A great investment for owners of small dogs is the Sherpa Bag, designed by former flight attendant Gayle Martz. With its hard bottom and soft, nylon-mesh sides, this airy, unique carry-on accommodates small dogs more comfortably than a standard crate. It even has side pockets for your vet's papers and dog toys! The Sherpa Bag is available at better pet boutiques or directly from **Sherpa's Pet Trading Co.**, 357 East 57th Street, #15A, New York, NY 10022, 212-838-9837. Prices range from $60 to $80.

When I fly with Serena, I don't board until I see the baggage handlers loading her. If the flight attendants try to urge me on board, I explain that I'm waiting to see my dog loaded and have always found them friendly and understanding.

Again, when booking your flights, think first of your pet's needs:

Travel early or late from warm destinations.

Fly directly whenever possible, making the trip as short as you can.

If you can't avoid a stopover, and need to change planes, make sure there is enough time between flights for your dog to be unloaded from the first plane and transported to and loaded on the next leg of the journey.

198

When you land at your destination, go directly to the baggage claim area to pick up your dog, and insist that he is delivered promptly to you! If you are not on hand in baggage claim, he could sit in his crate unsupervised. The best protection you have is to be present at the baggage claim area yourself to inquire after your dog if he is not delivered quickly.

When You Can't Be Home—Pet-Sitters and Boarding Kennels

At some point in your dog-owning career, you won't be able to get home in time to take care of your pet. You'll work late, you'll need to go away for a few days, or you'll go on a vacation. After you've exhausted the possibilities for imposing on friends or relatives, you'll need to seek professional help.

Depending on your area, your dog may have several options in your absence. He can be cared for by a professional pet-sitter/dog walker in your home, or you can send him to a boarding kennel.

PET-SITTING

The word "sitter" conjures up the image of a bored teenager watching TV and chatting on the phone while your dog chews through the baseboards. For this reason, pet-sitters often prefer to call themselves "in-home pet care providers."

In a pet-sitting arrangement your dog is cared for in the security of her own home. The in-home pet care provider

stops by several times a day to take your dog out, feed her, and spend time with her. This arrangement saves your pet the stress of being put in a kennel.

To get more information, and a list of pet-sitters in your area, contact the **National Association of Professional Pet Sitters,** 1200 G Street, NW, Suite 760, Washington, DC 20005, 202-393-3317. NAPPS provides members with accreditation, liability and bonding insurance, and has set forth a code of ethics. It also provides a mentoring program for people getting started in the business. Be careful, and check the references of any pet-sitter who is not a member of NAAPS.

BOARDING YOUR DOG

Since it is impossible to monitor what happens to your dog while she is at a kennel, you must be sure you are choosing a reputable establishment. Make sure the business is a member of the **American Boarding Kennel Association,** 4575 Galley Road, #400 A, Colorado Springs, CO 80915, 719-591-1113, or http://abka.com, which monitors and sanctions its members. You might also want to check with the local Better Business Bureau or veterinarians in the area.

Any kennel will require that your dog be current with his immunization shots. You will need to show written proof, which you can easily get from your vet's office. Be sure that you are comfortable with the veterinarian the establishment uses, or make it clear that you want your own veterinarian to

be called. Also supply the kennel with the phone number of a friend or relative who may be reached in case of an emergency.

Check to see which dog food they serve. It is better to send your dog along with a supply of his own food—for gastric continuity—as well as his favorite toys and his bed or the blanket he sleeps on. If your dog is on any medication, include enough of it for the entire stay, with specific instructions as to how and when it is to be administered.

Traditional boarding kennels are usually equipped with individual indoor/outdoor runs, meaning four- or five-foot-square fenced-in areas, generally with a bed and running water. These connect by a door to a longer five- by twenty-five-foot or so outside area. The dogs can go in and out during the day, but are closed inside at night. Frequently, a large common play area is used for training, or free time, where dogs can socialize.

With an indoor/outdoor run your dog is supposed to relieve himself in an inconspicuous corner of his indoor space or outside in the run. But some dogs don't catch on. They are so well housebroken that they won't "go" inside, and also consider the outdoor run like a patio. This is a problem. Kennel personnel are *supposed* to monitor the situation and leash-relieve these dogs. But even at the best place, on a busy weekend, the staff might *not* notice that your dog hasn't gone for two days and has a bladder the size of a football. Just to be safe, I suggest you pay the few dollars a day extra to have someone at the boarding kennel walk your dog.

You began by bringing home a wiggly pup, or by offering a second chance to an older pet. With your complementary companion at your side, you will both go through many phases and visit many places. As you do, remember to give to your dog what she gives to you: love and respect.

Appendix
Tools to Live Together
The Basic Commands, Household Manners, Crate Training, and Socialization

Training

You can begin to train your pet with six commands: **"Watch me," "Walking on leash—heel," "Come," "Sit," "Down,"** and **"Stay."** This is the elementary vocabulary you need to control your pet and form the foundation of a working bond. Puppy or older dog, this is where you start.

Working with you should be enjoyable for your pet. Make sure your training is positive and upbeat. Keep sessions short and always end on a successful note. Your dog will learn more in ten pleasurable minutes than in thirty boring ones.

There are four steps to teaching a dog anything. Using the command "sit" as an example:

Teach It

This is the elementary step of getting the dog to understand what you want him to do. If you want your dog to sit, hold a treat over his head as you say the word "Sit," or gently push his hind end down as you say the command until he associates the command with the action of his sitting.

Train It

Begin to reinforce the idea that when you say the word "sit" his hind end should go down. Practice what you have taught your pet several times a day with him on the leash so that you can correct a mistake.

Proof It

When you are sure that your dog has completely learned the command and can perform it without fail, you are ready to "proof" it: giving your pet the chance to execute the command in a situation where you cannot correct her.

Use It

Put all the pieces together and use the commands your dog has learned in her daily life. Rather than jumping up on a visitor, a pup trained to "sit" at the visitor's feet gets cooed over for how well behaved she is.

YOUR TOOLS

Begin your training with your dog or pup wearing a flat buckle collar. I like to use a six- or eight-foot-long leather leash because it is easier on the hands than either nylon or chain. For a thirty-foot line I prefer cotton webbing or a flexi-type lead.

Your dog's preference will determine what you use as a reward. If you are blessed with a pet who is so ball crazy that you can use a few seconds of play with a tennis ball as a reward, you are indeed lucky. The rest of us have to resort to food bribery. Use the smallest puppy biscuits, broken in half, as rewards. Some people also use little chunks of cheese, thin slices of hot dog, or desiccated liver as well.

TRAIN A TIRED DOG

Clearly, your pet needs enough energy to respond to you. But when you get home from work, a dog who has been sedentary for several hours needs to "blow off steam" and go to the bathroom before he can settle down to training. Don't try to work a dog who is all wound up. Take him for a run, or throw a stick for him for a while. Give him some time to "be a dog," stretching his legs and sniffing around all the new smells in the yard before you ask him to concentrate on you and your work together.

Once I have Serena's attention with a treat, I bring the snack up to my eye level, teaching her to "watch me" on command. *Courtesy of Jenny Eddy*

THE COMMANDS

Watch Me

Establishing eye contact with your pet is the foundation of working together. He must learn to turn his attention to you, no matter what else is going on in his environment. Even the tiniest puppies can execute this command for an instant.

Take either a treat or a ball in your hand. When he is in front of you, catch his attention with the treat. Say "Watch

me!" and slowly bring the treat up between your eyes to the middle of your forehead, just above your eyes. His eyes should follow the treat up to your eye level. When he holds his gaze on the object for a second or two, reward him with praise—a spoken "Good boy!," a pat, and the treat. After a free moment of play, try it again. Eventually, when you say "Watch me!" he will expectantly meet your gaze and respond to any subsequent command much more quickly. You can practice "Watch me!" at any time. In an instant it establishes an almost electric connection between you and your dog.

Walking on Leash—Heeling

Walking on leash is the first cooperative activity that you and your dog embark on, and it is the beginning of the training bond. You are asking him to focus on you and go where *you* choose, not where *he* chooses. It is also one of the many ways in which you can establish yourself as the leader in the relationship.

Accompanying a fellow pack member is one of the most instinctive canine behaviors. But the measured, steady pace and direct route that we humans prefer is foreign to a dog. Dogs were designed to trot or pace, not walk. They are much happier trotting, so you either need to walk very fast to keep up with your pet or train your pet to slow down.

Off leash and at liberty, a dog who was escorting you somewhere would fully experience the world around him. He would trot, walk, zigzag, and run, following a circuitous path determined by the interesting things he encounters along the way. He would check back with you en route and you would both end up in the same place. But he would have taken his own route, and you yours.

By adding the connection of the leash, you are asking him to stay with you and ignore most of the things that spark his fancy along the route. You also have changed the nature of the dog's accompanying you from his voluntary "Mind if I come along?" to your compulsory "You must come along." To make the process easier, your dog should be introduced to the leash as soon as possible: immediately, when you have a new puppy.

Never force a dog to move forward by pulling the leash. *Courtesy of Jenny Eddy*

TO START

Have your pet on your left side. In formal obedience classes, dogs stay on the left side of their owners when walking on the leash or "heeling," so you might as well accustom him to it. Be prepared with treats in your pocket.

Say your pet's name or give him the "watch me" command to get his attention. When he turns his focus to you, give him a cheerful command like "Let's go!" Step purposefully forward and start walking quickly. He may instinctively follow you. The instant he starts forward, encourage him verbally as you keep moving, "Good boy! That's it, let's go!"

If he doesn't instinctively follow you, let the leash tighten as you move forward. When it tightens his collar to the point where you feel mild tension, give him more verbal encouragement: "Come on, let's go." If he still doesn't budge, show him the treat or ball as an incentive. When he steps forward, give him lots of praise and encouragement for following you.

After several steps say, "Okay, halt," and stop. If he's paying attention to you, he should at least pause when you stop. Praise him in that instant and reward him with a treat. Repeat that process until he willingly follows you.

Always use encouragement and treats or toys to get your dog moving forward. Do not try to drag him. That will only frighten your pet, possibly to the point of panic when he feels the collar tighten on his throat.

With a squeak toy for encouragement, Sheltie Kate moves ahead easily. *Courtesy of Jenny Eddy*

DOGS WHO PULL

Some dogs immediately begin to pull when on a leash. Once they realize that going on the leash usually means an adventure, a dog can charge ahead in anticipation. Do not get in a pulling war with your dog, because you will lose. With their low centers of gravity, muscular backs, and powerful hindquarters, dogs are built to pull. Trainers describe a kind of biofeedback where the sensation of pulling against something stimulates a dog to pull even more.

Regain your dog's attention with a treat, then start walking, saying, "Let's go!" If he lunges ahead of you, pulling, immediately turn a quarter turn to your right, saying, "Here, boy." Don't jerk the leash, just make a ninety-degree turn and walk in that direction. When the few feet of leash becomes taut, your dog will be pulled after you. As he comes up beside you in the new direction, stop and give him a treat. Begin again the same way, turning ninety degrees if he charges ahead of you. Always give your pet the fair warning of a command like "come on" the instant you turn. This gives him the chance to heed your cue and not get pulled around.

Once your dog is moving easily with you on the leash, you can add some formal "heel" work. "Heeling" is far more structured than walking on the leash. The dog must stay on your left side, his shoulder even with your knee at all times. He must automatically "sit" when you stop. Practice this exercise by putting the command "heel" in place of your "Let's go" as you move forward, and adding your "sit" command when you stop. Soon your pet will automatically sit when you stop.

Come

This is the most important command, the one that might save your pet's life. Like walking on the leash, "come" taps directly into your dog's instinct to do things with his pack members. Wolves go places together. Similarly, whenever your dog follows you around the house he is "coming" with you. So by teaching your dog the "come" command, you are simply putting a name to a very natural canine behavior.

Start to introduce formal "coming" with your pet on her leash. Call her name in a happy voice, and say the command "Come!" The instant she turns her attention to you, start moving backward, away from her, calling her name excitedly. This backward movement will trigger her pack instinct and she will start moving toward you. As she comes forward, encourage her, saying, "Good girl, come!," reinforcing your command.

After four or five backward steps, move forward to meet her, bringing her to a stop with your body. Kneel down and give her a reward and lots of praise.

If she ignores you, say, "No! Come!," and start moving backward, making excited noises to get her attention. Your momentum will give her a jump start toward you when the leash becomes taut. The second she starts to follow, give her encouragement ("Good girl, come on!") and a reward when she finally reaches you.

After establishing the command on a short leash, graduate to your thirty-foot leash. You may need to jog backward to stay ahead of your dog. As she perfects her response, you can stop backing away from her. She should come up to you and sit in front of your knees to complete the exercise and earn her reward.

Stay

The more exuberant your pet is, the harder it will be to teach him this command, since it requires the dog to be still. Keep your "stay" lessons very short and conduct them at the end of a session, or after a run, when your dog is physically tired.

With your pet on the leash, have her "sit" in front of you. Use the "watch me" command to get her focused, then say, "Stay," as you swing your right arm, your hand flat, toward her face, stopping just before her nose. Take one step backward and stop still for a moment. If your backward momentum has not caused her to stand up and take a step forward, step back close to her with praise. Gradually increase the distance you move away from her until she will "stay" for several minutes with you four or five steps away from her at the end of her leash.

If she stands up to follow you when you step away, say, "No!," and move forward, toward her. Pull firmly up on her leash, putting her back in the sit position. Repeat the hand signal and the command "stay," stepping only a half step back this time.

The "stay" command can be challenging for dogs because it works against their instinct to follow you. Asking your pet to stay still while you step away or leave her can actually trigger separation anxiety. Proceed slowly, positively, and *very patiently*. You want to reassure her, not punish her.

"Stay" will become the command that places your dog peacefully at your feet while you watch television, or keeps her in one spot in the kitchen while you go in and out of the back door with the garbage. Many owners put their dogs on a half-hour down-stay (the owner can be working or doing something nearby) once a day as a subtle but effective way of reinforcing the owner's control of the pet.

Down

Begin with your dog sitting in front of you or at your side. Use the "watch me" command to get his attention and show him a treat or his ball. Bring the reward down to the floor in front of him, saying, "Down," as you do it. He should follow your hand, extending his front legs and lying down.

If he doesn't follow your hand, either lift his front feet and place him in the down position or exert downward pressure

Learning the "down" command: Serena willingly follows a treat to the ground and is rewarded. *Courtesy of Jenny Eddy*

with the leash. Say the command "down" so that he learns to associate the position on the floor with the verbal cue.

When he is "down," crouch next to him and reward him with praise and the treat. Keep him down for a second, then say, "Okay, sit," as you stand up, encouraging him into the sit position.

When he has learned to lie down on command, you can extend the amount of time he must stay on the floor. If he stands up, correct him with a "No! Down." You may need to stand next to him with one foot on the leash to prevent him from getting up. After a moment, release him with an "Okay, sit" and praise him.

"Down" should be put together with "stay." Gradually increase the length of time that the dog stays down until he can comfortably hold the position for several minutes.

Leave It

This will stop your dog from gobbling a dropped chicken leg or grabbing a shoe left out of your closet. Teach "leave it" with your dog on the leash and in the sit position. Place a treat on the floor in front of him as you say, "Leave it!" Hold the leash taut so that he is prevented from diving for the biscuit. Repeat "Leave it!" for a moment, then say "Okay!" as you release the leash, allowing him to eat the treat. Repeat this exercise, gradually extending the length of time that he must resist the treat.

These are the most basic commands, which will allow your pet to live with you in harmony.

A PRACTICE SESSION

A typical ten-minute training session might look something like this:

Three to four minutes of fast walking on the leash. Make several turns, reversals of directions, and stops. When this is going smoothly, practice "heeling" by having your pet "sit" each time he stops.

Four or five "comes." Put your dog on the thirty-foot leash and let him walk away from you as though at liberty. When his back is turned and the leash is slack, say his name and call him to "come." The instant he turns toward you, encourage him as you reel in the line. If he ignores your command, say, "No! Come!," and begin to reel him in anyway, praising him as he moves toward you.

One to two minutes of "heel" practice. Take two steps forward with your dog on the leash, stop and make him sit, reward, praise, two more steps and a sit.

Two to three minutes of "sit-stay" practice.

End with a minute or two of practicing the "down" command, combining it with a "stay" as your dog improves.

Ask your pet to "Watch me!" and "Leave it!" several times a day on an informal basis. Remember to end any training session on a positive note.

SELECTING A TRAINER OR CANINE BEHAVIORIST

In the past several years there has been an enormous philosophical split in dog-training theory. Masters like William Campbell, Ian Dunbar, Roy Hunter, John Fisher, Job Evans, and Carol Lee Benjamin have added a sensitivity to dog behavior to obedience training.

Their lead has been followed by a new generation of trainers who have rejected the old punishing methods of training dogs. These new "positive approach" trainers have broken ranks with those who continue to use harsh training tools such as shock collars, beatings, and hanging a dog in midair by using a choke chain. They focus their training on positive ways to teach the dog to behave, not forcing him into submission.

When selecting a trainer to work with, I beg you to find one who offers you positive guidance and preventive solutions to your dog's problems, *not harsh punishments*.

Your options for selecting a training program include: group obedience classes run at a center or in a park; a private trainer who will come to your home and work one-on-one with you and your dog; and canine behaviorists who deal with the more complex issues of dogs with chronic problems. Since your veterinarian is familiar with you and your dog, he will probably be able to suggest an area trainer to you. If you have a few names already, your vet's advice can help to narrow down the choices. You may also get information about obedience instructors in your area from **Robin Kovary** at **The American Dog Trainers Network Helpline,** 212-727-7257

(1–3 P.M. EST); **The Association of Pet Dog Trainers,** P.O. Box 3734, Salinas, CA 93912, 800-PET-DOGS; and **The National Association of Dog Obedience Instructors,** 2286 East Steel Road, St. Johns, MI 48879. Names of behaviorists are available from **Dr. Suzanne Hetts, Animal Behavior Associates,** 4994 South Independence Way, Littleton, CO 80123.

HOUSEHOLD MANNERS

Other Pets

Your new dog may need to learn to live with other creatures in your household. Whether these are cats, birds, or livestock, he must learn that these animals are members of your pack, not prey for him to chase.

Keep your dog on the leash when he meets his new animal family. Supervise his behavior, let them touch noses, but keep him calm. If the other pet is a cat, it is important to closely supervise the first few weeks together. Your kitty may simply disappear into a closet for several days. Eventually, your pets will work out a relationship, but protect the other animals by overseeing your dog's behavior during this process.

Children and Your Dog

Building a relationship with a dog is invaluable for children. They learn compassion for other living things and sensi-

tivity to the nonverbal communications of animals, and gain responsibility as they care for the pet.

"Oreo, meet Tucker, your new canine sister." Always have your dog on leash when making introductions. *Courtesy of the author*

    To help your dog get along with children, set ground rules for both of them. Train your pet not to play-bite or jump up. Explain to the children that just as humans do, dogs feel pain if they are poked or their fur is pulled; that screaming can hurt a dog's ears; and that dogs need time to themselves, when they can be left alone.

Supervise playtimes and monitor the excitement level. If play gets too rough, promptly take a time-out. Games of tag or tug-of-war may trigger a prey drive response in your dog, and he can easily become more excited than is appropriate. Break up the game and give your dog a few minutes to chill out in puppy central or in his crate. Let everyone calm down and then replace chasing and tugging games with retrieve games.

WATER SAFETY

Even though most dogs are natural swimmers, hundreds of pets die each year in water accidents. The most common calamity happens in the backyard swimming pool. Alone in the yard, a dog may slip or jump into the swimming pool and then be unable to get out. His struggling to get hold of the slippery sides quickly tires him out and, in exhaustion, he drowns.

Dogs and puppies must be trained to swim to the shallow end of the pool, or to the ladder to get out. If they do not receive this instruction, they are in danger. Make a point of giving your pet this life saving training and formally teach him to swim as I describe in chapter five, even if you do not plan to let him use your swimming pool.

When riding in a boat or swimming in the ocean, dogs should wear canine life preservers. Available through pet-supply catalogues, these are essentially chest harnesses with a buoyant material attached. They will keep your pet afloat if he falls off the craft or is sucked down by a strong undertow.

CRATE TRAINING

I believe that every dog should be crate-trained for his own safety and comfort. But you should never overuse your dog's crate. An hour or two at a time during the day is fine, or overnight when your dog would naturally be sleeping. But please do not sentence your pet to a life seen through the wire mesh of his crate door.

Always place your dog's crate in a central location to prevent him from feeling isolated and abandoned. This may mean carrying the crate into a corner of the kitchen for daytime use and back into the bedroom for the night.

Begin with the crate door open. Have a blanket and several of your pet's favorite toys inside. If you have an airline crate in two sections, you can even start with your dog becoming comfortable with the bottom half before you add the top.

Put a treat inside the crate, and encourage her to go inside with the command "In your crate." When she goes inside after the treat, praise her and reward her with a second treat. Let her come out, then try the command and treat again, always leaving the door open.

When your pup is accustomed to going in and out of the crate on command, you are ready to close the door. The best way is to give her a chew toy or a rawhide bone to ease the first experience. When she is inside with her treat, quietly close and latch the door behind her. Get up and resume what you were doing in the room, staying close by but not focusing on your pet. Do not say her name to reassure her, because she will think that you are calling her to come to you. When she realizes that the door is closed, she will probably paw at the door, whine, and even bark to be let out. Respond by saying, "No, quiet." The instant she is quiet you can open the door, releasing her. Never open the door when she is complaining, only when she is still.

This first experience should last no more than one minute. Leave the crate door open for an hour or so, encouraging her to go in and out, then repeat closing her in again for up to two minutes. Gradually increase her period of time inside the crate over the course of several days. Begin to briefly leave and return to the room as her periods of confinement get longer. Always praise her for going inside, correct her for barking, and reward her at the end of the exercise.

If you use the crate as your dog's nighttime place, next to your bed, introduce her to it in the afternoon and evening before her first night in the crate. When bedtime comes, give her a treat inside her crate. Close the door behind her and get into bed yourself. She may cry when the lights go out. Reassure her with a gentle "Quiet, good girl." You can even reach your hand down and let her lick your fingers through the wire. After a few minutes she should settle down and fall asleep.

A young puppy is likely to accept the crate with minimal complaining as long as you place it in an area where he still can see and hear you most of the time. Older dogs can be

more difficult to train. They may have preexisting issues with confinement and abandonment. Work slowly and calmly with these pets. If your dog won't accept the crate at all after a few weeks of careful, gentle introduction, you might want to consult a trainer or canine behaviorist.

SOCIALIZATION

Socialization gives your dog the social skills she needs to live in your world. Think of the various components of your life that will be unfamiliar to a dog. Each one must be introduced gently and positively for your dog to learn how to react to them.

From your first days together, make a point of exposing your pet to three or four new things a week, from fire engines in the street to the trapdoor that leads to your attic. Here is a list to start with.

Humans

Have your dog meet people of different ages and ethnic backgrounds, from babies in strollers to seniors with canes.

Places

Walk your pet on the leash around malls and downtown areas. Accustom her to the sounds, smells, and sights of busy streets as well as parks and forests.

Car Rides

Your dog doesn't even have to get out of the vehicle, she just needs to become accustomed to riding in the car with you.

Objects

There may be no stopping a determined terrier from attacking the vacuum, but at least you can try to introduce it to him reasonably. Also present blow dryers and other noisy appliances or tools in a gentle, positive manner.

Your dog will take his cue from your demeanor. Act happy and nonchalant when you introduce him to anything unfamiliar even if he shies away or barks in alarm. Have a pocket full of treats handy for positive reinforcement. If you are approaching a new person, have *that person* feed your dog the treat.